The Agile Brand

Creating authentic relationships between companies and consumers

by Greg Kihlström

Published by:

Yes&

1700 Diagonal Road, Suite 450

Alexandria, VA 22314

First Edition: May 1, 2018

The publisher is not responsible for websites (or their content) that are not owned by the publisher. All logos are property of their respective owners.

Edited by Anna-Marie Montague and Janelle Kihlström

Cover Design by Alicia Recco

ISBN - 978-1-54393-260-7

Contents

FOR EVERYONE WHO HAS TAUGHT ME
WHAT I KNOW ABOUT BRANDING & MARKETING.
THERE HAVE BEEN MANY.
THERE WILL BE MANY MORE.

Acknowledgements

As with any effort of this kind, there are many people I'd like to thank for their support and patience. While there are many more than those mentioned below, the following are a few without whom I could not have produced this book.

I'd like to thank the Carousel30 team for their support over the 14 years since I founded the company in December 2003 through the fall of 2017, when the company was acquired by Yes&.

My partners throughout the years there gave me the support to pursue things like writing books and other beneficial, though sleep-depriving endeavors: Brandon Prudent, Curtis Morehead, and Rohit Rao. In particular, Romie Stefanelli has been invaluable as a sounding board and counterpoint for some of my crazier ideas over the years.

Thanks to Alicia Recco for her wonderful work on the cover design and for creating all of the original illustrations for this book. Likewise, I'd like to thank everyone at Yes& for being such a great team to work with as I finished this book while completing the merger.

From Yes&, this would not have been possible without the support of the President and CEO, Bob Sprague, who was also kind enough to contribute the Foreword.

Anna-Marie Montague was invaluable to this effort as she helped shape some of the key parts of this book, and challenged me to go deeper on several points as she also edited it. Also, Bob Derby, with whom I've had a number of enlightening conversations and who helped particularly with the inflection point concept discussed in this book.

Gail Legaspi-Gaull of Hat Trick3C and Wendy Hagen of hagen inc. were greatly helpful in sharing their thoughts on the future of branding, and I've appreciated working with them on various branding projects over the years.

Lisa Nirell has remained an inspiration as I continue writing and speaking and I appreciate her thoughts on a draft of this book.

I also want to thank my sister, Janelle Kihlström Pomery, for her help in editing this book, and in untangling my initial words and thoughts into something which I hope marketers will find meaningful and helpful.

Finally, thanks to my wife Lindsey for her understanding of the many nights and weekends spent writing and researching this book, and for her support throughout the process.

"All things come into being through opposition and all are in flux like a river."

—Heroclitus, ca. 500 B.C.

Foreword

The Agile Brand. It sounds like an oxymoron. You know, like
"jumbo shrimp," or "military intelligence," or "Andrew Lloyd
Webber masterpiece."

I think most of us have thought of a brand – especially an
established consumer brand like Procter and Gamble, IBM, or
Ford – as something monolithic. Eternal. Something a company
builds over decades, until it achieves intrinsic value. A brand,
therefore, is to be guarded, protected, and preserved on all
fronts.

"Ha!' says Greg Kihlström in this entertaining and provocative
book. A brand that remains static in today's environment is an
anchor dragging its owner down. Today's consumers,
empowered through social media, online reviews, and other

phenomena of our digital age, want relationships with brands – and it's hard to have a relationship with a monolith. Instead, a brand must achieve agility – the ability to evolve over time in response to changing consumer tastes and market conditions.

But "agile" does not mean "wishy-washy," Greg further explains. A brand that is truly agile draws much of its strength from the permanent characteristics a company does or should maintain. Values. Mission. Purpose. It is this duality – roots in the eternal, relevance to today – that allows a brand to achieve agility, and to deliver its distinctive benefits.

This is what Jim Collins and Jerry Porras, in their seminal Built to Last, dubbed "the genius of the AND." Visionary companies, said Collins and Porras, preserve the core AND change the rest. (This was also partial inspiration for the name of the new agency Greg and his Carousel30 team have joined – Yes&.) Greg's thinking about brand provides us with a liberating principle: we need not choose between a brand that is responsive to change and one that has perpetual value: the Agile Brand is both.

How does one build an Agile Brand? Ah, you must read on. Greg's practical ideas and approaches fill these pages. Do not miss, however, his overriding message – one that I find both challenging and hopeful.

"Authentic" is a word that appears over and over in this book. The Agile Brand must be authentic, says Greg, or it is useless. Today's consumers are too savvy to be fooled for very long. No one, no matter how clever, creative, or well-funded, can build an agile brand on a lie.

Now contrast that, if you will, with the current political climate. As I write these words, our country has descended into an era in which it seems de rigeur for political leaders of all stripes to spout falsehoods and exaggerations daily. The fact checkers have thrown in the towel. Victory goes to he who lies loudest and longest.

Wouldn't it be deliciously ironic if we – the marketers, branders, and advertisers – began to be revered for our authenticity and truth telling? If consumers started to view our agile brands as particularly honest and trustworthy? (Our politicians and media have made the bar pretty darn low, believe me.)

I think we have the opportunity, through the Agile Brand, to build relationships in which consumers appreciate our efforts to make them aware of products and services that – authentically – would make them happy or improve their lives. I hope you, as I do, find Greg's ideas about the Agile Brand both powerful and refreshing.

Bob Sprague
February 2018

Introduction

"Your brand is a story unfolding across all customer touch points."
— *Jonah Sachs*

When I was way too young to drive anything but a bicycle (age 6 or 7), I became fascinated with cars. All kinds of cars. I drew them, read magazines about them, got my dad to take me to some car shows, and all in all, consumed a lot of information about them. This was well before the Internet was available (let's say early/mid-1980's), so most of what I consumed was printed materials like magazines.

There were so many styles and types of cars, and yet it became clear to me that there were certain car makes and models that seemed "right" for not only different *activities* (e.g., pickup trucks could haul all manner of things, and station wagons or minivans could transport kids to soccer games), but also for people with specific tastes.

When I think back, I was much less interested in how fast a Lamborghini could go from 0-60 miles per hour than what made it truly different from a Ferrari, and why someone would want one over the other. Or a Corvette, a Porsche – well, you get the picture. I guess I was a pretty lucky and/or spoiled kid (thanks Mom and Dad!) to at one point have had subscriptions to at least three different car-related magazines, and pick up a few British ones from time to time when I could convince my parents to add them to the cart. What I found on the pages of those magazines was a mix of advertising, opinion, and facts and figures. I got the story the car manufacturer wanted to tell, the experts' opinions, and the objective statistics and data, all in one.

Though at that young age I didn't have the vocabulary for it, the answers I was looking for came down to *branding.* On paper, there often wasn't a lot of difference between one mid-size sedan and another. After all, measurements like wheelbase or front seat headroom often varied only a little bit from the least expensive Chevy to the most expensive Mercedes. Instead, so much depended on the aesthetics of the car, the way it was portrayed in advertisements, its pricing tier, the story the company wanted to tell about its history and its customers, and all those other things that boil down to one thing: *branding*.

Ironically, I lost my interest in the minutia of all things automotive as I reached driving age, but my desire to better understand brands, branding, and our relationship with them was translated into many other areas of interest since then.

I joined a tech startup in 1999 that grew from zero to over a million users of what we would now call social networking or software as a service (SaaS) tools, and had the opportunity to build products for large brands like Coca-Cola, Lionsgate Films, and Amnesty International. All the software we created was centered on communications and connectivity, and though it pre-dated social media, we shared the same beliefs that brands can be more powerful when they connect with consumers, and allow consumers to connect with each other.

Around the end of the early 2000s tech boom, I was doing freelance creative for AOL, GEICO, Starbucks, and some smaller brands, and formed a digital agency called Carousel30. Over the next 14 years we built many new brands, grew existing brands, and created hundreds of marketing campaigns and websites.

Carousel30 gave me the chance to work with brands like Toyota, Porsche, United Nations, Abbott, VW, and many more, and to be awarded and recognized by some of the top names in the marketing and advertising industry.

Whether I was playing a strategy, design, or technology role, I always got the most satisfaction from the contributions my team and I made to organizations' brands, and in finding ways to connect them with their customers.

The importance of brands and branding

Let's face it. There are too many stimuli today, from the constant barrage of advertising on every device, medium and channel, to push notifications on your smartphone, to your flooding email inbox, and, well, you get the picture. Consumers with information overload need a way to make quick, informed decisions and choose the right product or service.

Just because a lot of content is being pushed to consumers doesn't mean that, beneath the noise, they aren't eager to solve their problems or find the things they want or truly need. Because of this, it is vital to have a strong brand that sets your company, your products and/or your services apart from your competition.

I also believe that brands can have a strong, *positive* influence on the world. Regardless of your political affiliation or socioeconomic background, the power, resources, and influence that a brand can have are extraordinary. With the right mission and values, anything from a one-person company to a multinational multi-billion-dollar corporation can have a tremendous effect.

So, what's missing?

If brands are so great, what is wrong? Or, to put it another way, with all the books, blog posts, podcasts, and other material about branding, why another book?

Although there are many books on branding, I felt a need to write about a dawning era of branding and brands' relationships with consumers. This book will focus on what the *new* brand, the *agile* brand is, where it originated, and where branding as a discipline, and an interaction between companies and consumers, is going. While many successful brands have found ways to interact with customers in creative ways for decades through fan clubs, product demos, publicity events among other ideas, there is something different about the brands of the present and future.

Today, we as marketers are creating living, interactive relationships with our customers that extend well beyond a recognizable name and mark.

These consumer-brand relationships are also based on product benefits which go beyond the superficial and difficult to prove (i.e., drinking Pepsi will make you happier, or driving a Corvette will make you feel younger), and are more authentic, measurable, and genuine. We will explore what a brand means and how it behaves almost as an organism with a life all its own, and how, with the right kind of direction, care and feedback loop, it can become benefit everyone around it: customers, shareholders, and the world at large.

Who this book is for

Anyone interested in brands may find some engaging nuggets, but this book is primarily for marketers, brand managers, and others who work on behalf of an organization to maintain and grow one or more *brands.*

My goal is to illustrate how the evolution of brands has both *shaped* and *been shaped by* our culture and society. It is also for the marketer who needs to understand where brands and branding are headed, and for the branding professional who needs to understand how the latest in agile marketing affects how brands operate.

This book is not intended to be a branding primer. We won't be discussing how to design logos or name companies, nor describing the proper way to write a mission or positioning statement. While it is not about agile software development practices, it touches lightly on how this shift in development influenced agile marketing, to paint the picture of what we mean when we say, "the agile brand." The book also includes some basic branding definitions and precepts as context for why brands are evolving and the purpose that these new, agile brands play in our society.

What we're going to discuss

Part 1 will provide the background for our journey through the new brand with context and background on how we've gotten where we are today.

Part 2 will discuss what we mean when we use the term "agile" and how the agile brand has come to be, its place in the current marketing environment, and the future of branding.

Part 3 focuses on the future of the consumer-brand relationship and where we go from here.

Enough with the setup. Let's get started with an introduction to the vocabulary we will use for brands and branding.

Part 1
The Basics of Brands

"A brand is the set of expectations, memories, stories and relationships that, taken together, account for a consumer's decision to choose one product or service over another."
—Seth Godin

1 | What Is Branding?

"Your brand is what other people say about you when you're not in the room."
–Jeff Bezos, Amazon

The following is my definition of branding, and I'll revisit several of these concepts later in discussing the agile brand.

Your brand is a vocabulary

Kleenex is more than a brand. It's an object and its name has replaced the word "tissue" in many people's minds. Similarly, when you search for something online, you "Google" it. In many places, if you want any type of soda, it's a "Coke." These brand names have infiltrated our minds and have come to mean something much beyond a single product. Scientists use an implicit association test (IAT), first introduced in 1998[1], to measure the strength of a person's automatic association between mental representations of products, objects, or abstract concepts in their memories.

Is it a Kleenex or a tissue? Image courtesy of Wikimedia Commons.

This tests the degree to which people's associations with the connotations of a specific word are more likely to be personal and subjective, rather than superficial and objective. For instance, the word "dog" may bring to mind a specific German

Shepherd that your neighbor had when you were 14 years old, not some generic image of a dog.

Branding is the vocabulary you use to teach others about your company, your product, or the services you provide, and it can paint a *lasting* picture in their minds. Your customers, current or potential, need to be taught how you would like them to talk about you.

With word of mouth being such a critical channel for brands to gain awareness, whether in the real world or on social media, review sites, or other online properties, it is critical to help consumers by teaching them the words, benefits, and other attributes that define your brand.

This vocabulary includes several concepts that are important to define for your audiences, such as what you do, how you do it, and the key selling points that your biggest fans can use to convince their family, friends and colleagues to try, switch to, or buy your product or services, support your cause or whatever your brand represents.

Remember, if you don't define these things for your audience, they will do it for you, and their representations will not always be the way you'd like to be known.

Let's take something as simple as pronunciation of a brand name. Below are a few examples of some popular brands, common mispronunciations, and correct pronunciations[2]:

Brand Name	Common Mispronunciation	Correct Pronunciation
Adidas	Uh-DEE-das	AH-dee-das
Hermes	Her-MEES	AIR-mez
Ikea	Eye - Key – Uh	Ee -Kay - Uh
Porsche	POORSH	POOR-sha

If people are doing something as fundamental as mispronouncing your company name, think of the missed opportunities if they don't understand the subtler aspects of your brand, such as your mission or unique selling proposition.

To teach consumers your brand vocabulary takes time, repetition, and a strategy that ensures you are hitting the same points consistently with the same audiences.

Your brand is more than a logo

Some who are new to branding might be confused by the fact that a logo is only one element among many brand aspects.

Over time, brands have become increasingly complex, with additional components. For instance, with the advent of the Web, an organization's website, social media voice, and any number of digital marketing elements have now become vital parts of its brand.

Your brand is a relationship

Brands have become understood as more than something you can see on a printed page or a digital platform. They are living, breathing organisms that you can gain experiences from, and they are entities which consumers are able to have a relationship with. This is the essence of the new brand, the agile brand, which is the focus of this book.

While in some sense this has always been the case, more recently, with the advent of channels and venues that allow brands to have real-time and persistent interactive communication with consumers, this notion of brand relationships has become both deeper and more pervasive.

Prior to being able to tweet in real-time with a brand, consumers still felt relationships with brands, but it was often one-sided, and fairly one-dimensional. A brand fulfilled a specific need or purpose, and when that need was filled, the relationship was often put on "pause" until the need arose again. For instance, forty years ago, if you were thirsty for Coca-Cola, the solution was simple: buy a bottle of Coke. Once you bought the bottle and consumed it, your "relationship" was on hold until you wanted more of the beverage. The way around this was to plaster the Coca-Cola name everywhere it could be seen, but in a world where every brand takes the same approach, simply having your name or logo visible isn't enough to keep you top of mind.

With the advent of communication tools such as social media, this relationship became a lot more bi-directional, or even omnidirectional since others could share in a conversation between one consumer and a company.

Your brand is continually evolving

There is one thing you can safely say: the relationship between brands and consumers is continually changing and evolving. Just as brands grow more sophisticated over time, so do consumers' relationships with them.

Suffice it to say, a successful brand is one that is able to achieve the duality of staying true to its values and mission, while evolving and adapting to new trends, preferences, tastes, and ideas over time.

While this may seem like a paradox, it is the standard by which brands are judged.

Recap

While the term "branding" can be used to mean a lot of things, a brand is much more than a name, a logo or a set of guidelines. It has grown over time into something more akin to a living organism capable of establishing and maintaining relationships with multiple people, and this will continue to evolve over time.

2 | Why Do We Brand?

"At the heart of branding is the promise that is made by the organization to the audience. The brand promise tells the audiences who you are, what you believe in, and what unique value you provide. The ability to fulfill your promises at every stage of the relationship is the defining factor for most organizations' success or failure. When promises are broken the reputation of the organization is called into question, and the brand suffers. When brand promises are kept, audiences respond with loyalty and affection."

—Melissa Mazzoleni, "4 Key Reasons Why Branding is Important", HOW Magazine

The purpose of branding

There are several reasons branding is so important:

1. Differentiation and Competitive Advantage
2. Value Creation for the Organization
3. Expectation Setting for Customers
4. Attracting the Right Employees

Differentiation and competitive advantage

The most obvious and visible reason for a unique brand is that it clearly differentiates you from your competitors. The McDonald's golden arches are visual shorthand for a number of brand attributes that set it apart it from Burger King, Wendy's, Arby's, Taco Bell and the entire slew of fast food competitors. From a very practical perspective, a strong brand helps you get noticed, and provides instant recognition for those already familiar with your brand.

But beyond allowing your sign to stand out on the side of the highway, there are other benefits to clear differentiation

Not only does a unique brand help a consumer see why your products and services are special, valuable, or relevant to them, it also gives them the words, phrases, and talking points they can use when their friends, colleagues, or family ask them about your brand. Clearly differentiating your brand makes it easy for everyone to understand why you are right for them.

Creating value for the organization

A strong brand can be an asset unto itself. Whether it is its licensing value, the ability to sell franchises, or simply the cachet that it adds to any products, services, or initiatives that you may be involved in, a great brand can be a multiplier for anything you want to accomplish.

This brand value can be leveraged in many ways, from providing the foundation to move into a new market, launch a new product, or even to transition from a private company to a public one through an IPO.

Setting customer expectations

To go back to the McDonald's example, when you see the golden arches, you immediately know what to expect. You won't be able to order a medium rare steak that was sourced from a local farm. Instead, you'll be able to order a Big Mac and other familiar McDonald's menu items.

Branding is the reason people understand this. They've seen the commercials, most likely been to allocation, or, according to Eric Schlosser in Fast Food Nation, if they are one in eight workers in the United States[3], they've been employed by the fast food restaurant at some point in their career.

A strong brand is not only recognizable to those familiar with it, it also sets expectations about quality and service to those who are not yet acquainted. For instance, by comparing the outside of an Old Navy clothing store with the exterior of Hermes or Louis Vuitton, you will most likely be able to tell a lot about the quality, price, and experience you will have in one shop versus another. It doesn't take a deep knowledge of their brands or pricing structure to help you immediately differentiate between them and determine which might be what you are looking for. To take this a step further, just as Old Navy and Hermes can be easily distinguished by their *class* of brand, so do Hermes and Louis Vuitton need to distinguish themselves amongst one another within the *same* brand class.

Attracting the right employees

We have been talking quite a bit about the *external* aspects of branding, but there are many internal benefits to a strong brand as well. Strong values help attract the right type of employees, and play a part in defining company culture.

Jose Gonzalez talks about this "employment brand"[4] in the following way:

> "Your company has an employment brand, whether you do anything with the brand or not. Whether you think you're branding yourself, or you're talking about your employment brand, it exists. It exists with your current employees and what they're telling people and sharing with their friends and family or connections. It exists with former employees."

For example, in my former agency, Carousel30, we wrote our values on one of our many chalkboard walls. It served as a continual reminder of what we stood for, and why we did what we did. Our values included our promise of quality for work we performed, as well as the relationships we had with each other, our clients, and our partners.

A clear, concise brand makes it easy for your employees to tell others what you do and allows them to become some of your best brand ambassadors. This can help new customers or prospective employees find you, especially when their expectations are clearly managed. Instead of relying solely on a sales person or on executives to engage in conversations about your brand, providing your employees with this type of information and material increases your salesforce and networking capabilities dramatically.

Recap

The purpose of a brand is more complex than simply triggering name or product recognition. An effective brand sets your company apart from the competition, and establishes an expectation with both new and existing customers of what they can will experience when they interact with our products, services, and people.

3 | What Makes a Brand Successful?

"Brands are psychology and science brought together as a promise mark as opposed to a trademark. Products have life cycles. Brands outlive products."
—*Scott Goodson, Founder, StrawberryFrog*

There are three primary ways to measure the success of a brand:

1. Substance
2. Focus
3. Relevance

Substance

For a brand to be strong and have lasting success, it must have substance. We can describe substance in two ways: 1) an ideology which is clearly articulated in the way an organization conducts business and communicates with its audiences, and 2) a genuine experience for the brand's audiences that builds a memorable and meaningful relationship.

Let's talk about ideology and brands first.

Brands that occupy an ideology can endure even as tastes and fads change. They can endure changes in products, in technology, and in generational preferences if they can exist as something deeper than what is visible to the eye.

Patagonia is a great example of a brand that has kept pace with change while remaining true to its ideals. Started in 1973 by Yvon Chouinard, the company sold a limited number of products targeting those who love the outdoors. Four decades and 30 stores later, Patagonia does nearly a billion dollars in sales[5]. How did this happen? Patagonia has remained true to both a simple design philosophy and its support for environmental advocacy.

While its products have expanded to clothes and gear for skiing and surfing and even a branded craft beer, Patagonia's success can be attributed to never deviating from its environmental values.

Offering a great experience

Substance also means delivering an authentic brand experience to your customers. It's not enough to offer a good product at a good price. This goes beyond competitive marketplaces, which have obviously existed for centuries. With the almost infinite amount of customization available, niche products, and delivery methods, consumers continue to expect more of what they want, when and how they want it.

For example, it's not good enough to have a great hotel room. What happens when something goes wrong? I was recently staying at a Hyatt Regency and having issues watching Netflix through the TV (a feature the brand touts). One message to the hotel Twitter account later, and someone was actively working to solve my problem. To me, that is a great experience, because I hate using the phone. For someone else, a great experience might entail a more hands-on approach. A brand that understands that different people have different preferences and can tailor an experience to each will win loyal customers.

Timelessness

When you think of some of the greatest brands, they have maintained a timeless aspect, regardless of aesthetic refreshes from time to time. Brands like IBM, Apple, and Coca-Cola have had great staying power because their core values have remained constant. While there are many factors at play, this timelessness is due in great part to the fact that the brands have built substance over time.

This timelessness can be attributed to understanding the dichotomy between having a strong mission, values and sense of purpose which *doesn't* change, and the flexibility to be agile as preferences change, trends come and go, and generational shifts occur.

Focus

"Our audience is everyone." If I had a nickel for every time I've heard that sentence after asking a marketer or executive, I'd be a very rich man.

As a consultant, I've dealt with many types of organizations, from Fortune 50 brands, to small nonprofits with a handful of staff. One issue that plagues an alarming number of them is *lack of focus on their core audience*. Any brand, no matter how large, how broad-reaching, how useful their products or services may be to a wide population, must have focus to succeed.

Let's take Apple as an example. It's true that the iPhone is popular with a wide variety of demographics around the world. Apple has sold nearly 1.2 billion phones[6] since they were introduced in 2007. That makes it a very successful product.

But what makes the iPhone so successful is that Apple has always had a focus on what it was, what its strengths are, and an understanding of who its target audience is.

While we don't have access to the internal memos and documents that may shed a more specific light on this, there are a few things that we can assume. The iPhone is targeted at rather narrowly defined audience, yet it is *because* of this narrow focus that it is so appealing. Apple has aimed at delivering a premium product which is easy to use. This means that it is priced as if its sole target is a well-educated, higher-income consumer, yet this is not the only demographic buying the product.

Relevance

Finally, in order for a brand to be strong, it must remain relevant or find a way to be culturally relevant in the moment.

Why has McDonald's survived through the decades when so many other brands and products have not? One reason is that McDonald's has remained fast. Though tastes shift, and even the term *fast food* has fallen out of favor (see: quick service), one constant in our culture is that we always see ourselves as busy and short on time. If and until this changes, McDonalds' focus on speed remains important.

Or take Lego, which was founded in 1939 and has found ways to reinvent itself over the decades to remain relevant. Whether it was the opening of the first Legoland in 1968, drawing over 650,000 visitors in its first year, or the release of their first feature film, *The Lego Movie*, in 2014, which drew a $400 million box office[7], the brand has expanded its offerings and focus but never lost touch with what makes its product successful.

For Lego, staying relevant meant expanding its targeting by finding ways to attract adults to want Legos for themselves (not just for their children) by the early 21st century. This, along with some successful tie-ins with properties such as Star Wars and Batman, let Lego keep itself culturally relevant, while reintroducing itself and its products to an age segment which had discarded it because they felt they'd outgrown Legos.

It's not enough to simply (or not so simply) create an agile brand. You need to build a *successful* one as well. Now that we've discussed the process and pieces that make up the agile brand, let's discuss what the measurements of success are.

Recap

Your brand is the way your audience sees you, how they remember you, and how they share your story with others. Your brand takes on meaning from the interactions you have with your customers. A successful brand has multiple dimensions that translate strong visuals to ideas, experiences, and feelings that extend beyond a single interaction.

To be a truly successful brand demands vigilance in maintaining the substance, focus, and relevance necessary to keep a close relationship with your audiences

4 | The Evolution of the Brand-Consumer Relationship

"We live in a Brand Era, where branding is in, and for some, aspiring to the Paul Rand style of logo craftsmanship is about as hip and contemporary as writing your invoices with a quill. Yes, logo design is only one facet of the powerful force that we call brand identity. The history of logo design begins with the roots of human expression."
—Dan Redding, Smashing Magazine

Being a great brand marketer means having a full understanding of how consumers interact with and experience brands. It also means you know and appreciate how the discipline has evolved over the years, as well as how consumers interact with companies, products, and causes. While some fundamentals never change, it's important to understand how brands have evolved in the eyes of both marketers and their audiences over the years.

We can look at the evolution of brands as encompassing four eras, each of which we'll review in more detail:

1. Brand as object
2. Brand as idea
3. Brand as experience
4. Brand as relationship

As you work tirelessly to create an engaging experience between your audiences and your brand, keep this evolution in mind. You can also look at these as four dimensions that your brand needs to exist within. Remember that none of these dimensions have become irrelevant, even as brands' relationship with consumers has evolved. Instead, it's an additive process. Over time, brands have become more complex, with each new evolution adding a new layer of meaning and understanding. Now, let's get started.

Brand as object

"Identities are the beginning of everything. They are how something is recognized and understood. What could be better than that?"
—*Paula Scher*

BRAND AS OBJECT

AWARENESS   **ACTION**

Name, company, and/or product recognition translates to sales

Our use of logos to represent companies, organizations, or individuals is based on a long history that originates with the very beginning of written communication. The moment we used a drawing, an image, a symbol to represent *something else*, we've been essentially branding things. From cave paintings to hieroglyphics, to the first logo representing a company, we've been using graphic representations to give meaning to ideas.

45

Dan Redding puts it this way[8]:

> *"Signs can take the form of words, images, flavors, or even odors: things that have no intrinsic meaning until we invest it in them. We perceive, understand, and negotiate the world around us by investing meaning in all manner of signs and symbols. In the West, an image of a snake signifies evil. But without our Western cultural and mythological associations (many of which are rooted in the Bible), a serpent is just a serpent."*

The Stella Artois logo, first used in 1366, is the earliest known logo.

In the early days of marketing and advertising, it was enough to simply have name or product recognition in order to generate sales. Mass advertising created mass sales.

With a proliferation of logos comes the need for brands to find ways beyond just a name and logo to differentiate themselves. (Image courtesy of Wikimedia Commons)

Brand as idea

"Brand: Is not logo, not what it looks like when I look at your product. A Brand is a shortcut, it's a shortcut for all the expectations I have for what you're about to do for me. It's a shortcut for trust, for promises, for conversations. A brand that's worth something, is worth something either because you can sell more of it, or make more of a profit for each one you sell. That's it. If you can't sell more, or can't get a premium, you don't have a

brand. Cause people aren't showing up investing their emotion in what it is you sell."
—*Seth Godin*

Perception of the products or company and the feelings and ideas they evoke translate to sales

With increasing competition from mass production, mass advertising, and mass media in general, the need for brands to be more than an object came along. At this point, it wasn't enough to simply have a logo that was recognizable and a product that was available in stores.

Brands now needed to compete for mindshare, or as Will Burns says in his article on Forbes.com, "Branding is what happens to people after they've spent time interacting with your company."

As consumers and marketers have grown more sophisticated, it is not enough to simply be known. Companies and products must stake out a claim on an area of the popular imagination and exist as an "idea."

For instance, seeing the "golden arches" of McDonald's plants an idea in your head. Maybe it's a Big Mac, fries, or a large Coca-Cola. Whatever it is, (and whatever your feelings about its products), that yellow "M" brings with it more than just an opinion of yellow on red typography.

The same applies to Starbucks, who were so successful with their previous branding recognition efforts that they removed the word "Starbucks" from their logo and suffered no discernable setbacks.

Brand as experience

> *"A brand is no longer what we tell the consumer it is—it is what consumers tell each other it is."*
> *—Scott Cook*

BRAND AS EXPERIENCE

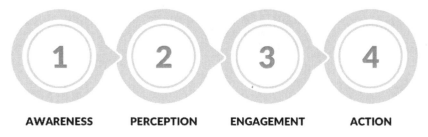

| AWARENESS | PERCEPTION | ENGAGEMENT | ACTION |

Customers' interactions with brands build deeper connections which translate to sales

With increased competition, and consumer preference for more tailored products and services, brands were forced to differentiate themselves beyond occupying an idea. They needed to insert themselves into key life moments and become part of our experience.

Going back to an earlier brand example, Apple's brand experience extends all the way from the initial sale (either in one of its branded stores or its online presence), through the packaging you open to first use your product, through the ease of setup, through usage of the product every day. And if you have problems, you can go to the Apple Store to ask questions.

In more recent times, brands have used experience to cut through the clutter of marketing and advertising, which creates deeper engagement with customers.

Brand as relationship

"Too many companies want their brands to reflect some idealised, perfected image of themselves. As a consequence, their brands acquire no texture, no character and no public trust."

—Richard Branson, Founder of Virgin Group

INITIAL CUSTOMER EXPERIENCE

LONG-TERM CUSTOMER EXPERIENCE

As more and more brands have adopted the experience approach, it has become clearer that a one-off moment in time is not enough to cement brand loyalty. This takes us to the current stage in the evolution of brands: brand as relationship.

Mark Bonchek and Cara France have a great take on this in their article in Harvard Business Review:

To get started, think about the relationship people have with your brand today. Frame your answer as social roles. For example, if you are a healthcare provider, you probably have a brand relationship based on doctor/patient. Now think about other kinds of relationships outside your industry. For example, in health care there are aspects of teacher/student   (to educate), coach/athlete (to motivate), or guide/traveler (to navigate). Be sure to consider roles that are symmetrical, like friend/friend, neighbor/neighbor or co-creator/co-creator.

Now that just about every brand is on social media, and has some type of interactive presence, it's not enough to simply be available and able to be searched and found. It's also not enough to have a one-off experience with a customer.

In order to truly build long-term value with a customer, you need to consider the type of relationship you can realistically have with your audiences and build on that. This takes understanding the type of relationship your customers want to have with *you* and designing an experience around it. It also takes a holistic approach to your customer experience that goes beyond single channels, devices, or events. By thinking in terms of a long-term relationship, instead of short-term wins, your brand takes on a new life, and a cohesive multi-channel strategy takes on even more importance than ever.

According to a recent study by Epsilon[9], 80% of consumers said they are more likely to buy from a company if their experience is personalized. Your customers may not always be ready to purchase, but by keeping them engaged, they'll be more likely to buy from you when they are.

It is also important to understand that, while a customer might be loyal, they might not always be in the "buying" mood. So, smart marketers have learned how to nurture customers and keep them in a state of engagement, even while they may not always be ready to take action. This state of engagement also means that they will be primed to refer your brand to their friends and colleagues when the time comes. Word of mouth occurs from engaged customers, and makes a huge difference to brands that are able to achieve a loyal following.

Recap

While brands have evolved from a simple mark to a lifestyle experience, this has been an additive process. It's not the case that brands have simply "skipped" over to the last step of brand evolution. Instead, as time goes on, the practice of branding has become more nuanced. Because of this, we need to think of brands in terms of all four dimensions, not just a single one.

Part 2
The Agile Brand

"Our job is to connect to people, to interact with them in a way that leaves them better than we found them, more able to get where they'd like to go."
—Seth Godin

5 | What Changed?

"The difference between winning and losing is he who treats the customer the best."
—*Mark Hurd, Oracle*

Over time, brands evolved from graphic symbols to having much more complex interactions with consumers, going from object, to idea, and then from experience to relationship.

We can look at this evolution as the result of four phenomenon:

- **Social Transformation**
  Social media, in its broadest sense, has transformed commerce, marketing, media relations, and our relationships with both brands and our colleagues, friends, and family.

- **Brand as Relationship**

  Unlike the "Mad Men" days of advertising, it's not enough to send one-way messages. Successful brands don't talk *at* people, they engage *with* them. A modern brand offers a multi-channel customer experience that is a persistent two-way exchange, more like a relationship than a one-off experience.

- **Device-agnostic Consumers**

  Customers are device-agnostic, always-connected, and want personalized relationships with brands. Successful brands understand that customers want *what* they want, *when* and *where* they want it.

- **Data Driven Decision Making**

  Data is readily available and plentiful, which empowers businesses to make quicker decisions that are informed by real-time information.

Let's look at each of these concepts in more depth.

Social transformation

How do you learn about new products and services? If you asked someone 30 years ago, their answers would have been vastly different. In the 1980s, there were a few common ways that you might have learned about a product:

- In conversation with friends, family & neighbors
- Television or radio ads
- Magazine or newspaper ads
- Direct Mail
- In-store product displays
- Billboards or signs

Note that none of these media have ceased to exist. If anything, spending on television, in particular, continues to increase, albeit slowly these days[10], despite online advertising overtaking it in terms of overall spending in 2017.

But while all of these media exist, think about the first item above in particular. Conversations with friends, family and neighbors took place by phone or in person 30 years ago. With the advent of email, instant messaging, text messaging and, social media, the way we interact with one another has completely changed.

What about the power of consumer reviews? In 1936, a nonprofit group called the Consumers Union started a publication[11] that sought to put power in the hands of individuals to help one another in an era where there were few consumer protection laws. It was so influential, for instance, that Minnesota Congressman John Blatnik credited the magazine in 1958[12] with holding tobacco companies accountable for misleading consumers about the claims that filter-tip cigarettes diminished tar and nicotine intake.

This publication was called *Consumer Reports* and its role in shaping the consumer-brand relationship is undeniable. As other sources of reviews have increased, most notably from Amazon but quickly followed by others, *Consumer Reports'* subscriber numbers have declined from a peak of nearly 8 million in 2008 to about 7 million as of mid-2016.

In addition to consumers having online and asynchronous types of communication and relationships with others, they increasingly rely on strangers' opinions as well. Instead of a handful of sources like *Consumer Reports*, you now see reviews and ratings systems everywhere you look, with many retailers allowing feedback (both good and bad) on their own sites. Through online reviews and ratings systems, we have the instant gratification of asking someone for advice whenever need an opinion and wherever we are.

This social transformation is already fodder for many books, but it's important to note in talking about brands. The new meaning of "word of mouth" as well as how the dissociated and asynchronous nature of our communication cause us to interact, trust, and connect in ever evolving ways.

Brand as relationship

Is Nike *just* a shoe company? Does Disney *just* make movies? When does a brand transcend a set of one-off experiences with its customers and become a true part of their lives?

Launched in May of 2006[13], Nike+ made the brand much more than a shoe company. With the iPhone launching a little over 12 months later, the Nike+ was a first of its kind activity tracker that tied the Apple iPod to Nike products via a sensor. The Nike+ app was updated continuously to take advantage of the iPhone and its features, and by April 2013 had 18 million users[14].

While we may take this functionality for granted, (it was later embraced by Fitbit, as well as Apple itself on its Watch), the close tie-in between Nike's traditional product set and the activity that its customers engaged in was a breakthrough. Forget how cool it was that the iPod and later iPhone could track activity, or the hours and millions of dollars of development that went into that technology. Those devices were and are just a means to an end. Nike's end game was to be synonymous with the *experience* its customers had when using its products.

Disney, to a greater extent, has built its brand into an empire of immersive experience, and has a head start over most brands. Following the bankruptcy of his first animated endeavor[15], Walt Disney moved to Hollywood and started what would become The Walt Disney Company in 1923. The company started creating its own worlds with animated short, features and television shows. It then expanded to even more immersive forms of entertainment. From theme parks (the first of which opened in 1955), to movies, to cruise lines, stores in shopping malls, and a television *network*, Disney has continued to embrace *experience* wherever it can. This includes interactive experiences through games and the Web, and I'm sure it will continue as long as there are new media to venture into.

Additionally, Disney, seeing that many of its characters and stories would not appeal to older generations, has invested billions of dollars in production companies like Pixar and franchises such as Marvel and Star Wars, in order to expand its audiences.

In fact, Disney has invested so much in brand relationship and customer experience, it has created a Customer Experience Summit which helps teach other brands how to use similar approaches to reach their audiences.

While Nike's and Disney's "products" are very different, their embrace of brand as relationship sets them apart from competition that doesn't form a long-term bond with their customers.

Device-agnostic consumers

A discussion of customer experience merits its *own* book, but let's talk about customer experience in terms of customer service.

How many ways can you interact with Amazon?
- Send a message through their website
- Ask Alexa to contact (through your Amazon Echo or other device)
- Send a Tweet or direct message through Twitter

- Message them on Facebook

And yes, if you look hard enough, you can even talk with someone from Amazon on the *telephone!* While this might sound particularly facetious, how about trying to call another well-known organization on the phone? My car was recently damaged in a hit and run accident while parked right outside the front of my house. My insurance is through GEICO, and I've always told others how great their customer service is, and how easy it is to talk with them when I need something. It turns out I have only really needed GEICO to sign up for new insurance, or switch it from one car or another.

So, while I sat mourning the loss of my nearly brand-new Audi S5's front end, I thought it would be easy to call GEICO and report the accident. Several minutes later, I discovered that they make it nearly impossible to report an incident through any method other than their app or a website if you are using your smartphone. In this case, I was frustrated, waiting for police to arrive, and not eager to download an app; and would have appreciated the ability to call instead.

Customers demand instant solutions that utilize the platform that makes the most sense at that moment. While some people have a more constant communication preference, most consumers are changing to a more channel-agnostic approach to customer service requests.

Someone who is at the airport with only a mobile phone is not going to try to submit a website form request, or even spend the time to search for a customer service number. They may turn to Twitter because it's readily available. But the same customer might use a company's website to send a request at home, sitting on the couch with their tablet or laptop. Responsive customer experience demands that companies provide multiple parallel methods contact and of delivering great customer service.

And this just touches on customer *service.* What about your e-commerce experience, or the way that you market to and communicate with customers?

Data-driven decision making

How do you make marketing decisions? We'll discuss this topic further when we explore agile marketing. Let's briefly look at some of the ways that even small businesses are gaining insights that simply weren't available several decades ago:

- Real-time analytics
- Artificial Intelligence
- Business intelligence (BI) tools

Access to tools that enable data-driven decision making has empowered organizations of all kinds to utilize real-time information in their marketing strategy, planning, and execution.

This ability to read and report on up-to-the-minute information and the number-crunching capabilities of many data platforms puts enormous power in the hands of businesses and marketers. In a few chapters, we'll talk about how this led to the rise of agile marketing.

Recap

Shifts in consumer behavior and technology have shaped both our relationship with brands, and the way that those brands seek to have relationships with their customers. Branding has followed and will continue to follow the trends and behaviors of the rest of society over time, and I'm sure that in twenty years we'll have a new list of (at least) four items which have shaped how brands present themselves and interact with consumers!

6 | What is Agile?

"The more they overthink the plumbing, the easier it is to stop up the drain."

– Scotty, Star Trek III: The Search for Spock.

Introduction

To complete our discussion of what we mean by an "agile brand", we need to explain exactly what we mean by the term agile. Merriam Webster defines it as[16]:

1: marked by ready ability to move with quick easy grace: an *agile* dancer

2: having a quick resourceful and adaptable character: an *agile* mind

History of agile

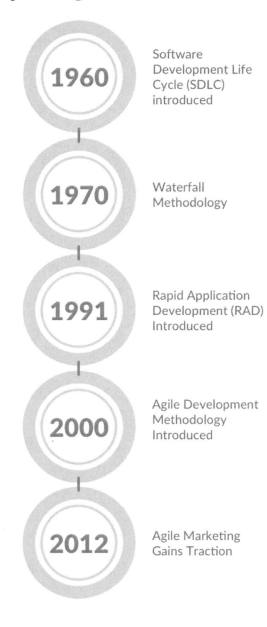

1960 — Software Development Life Cycle (SDLC) introduced

1970 — Waterfall Methodology

1991 — Rapid Application Development (RAD) Introduced

2000 — Agile Development Methodology Introduced

2012 — Agile Marketing Gains Traction

While these are not too far off, we are referring to computer programming methodologies developed in the late 1990s and refined and defined in the early 2000s.

Agile methodology, which we'll discuss in more detail shortly, opened the doors to many of the products, startups and technologies that we use today. It's amazing what difference an approach to writing code can have on our lives!

In full disclosure, I've taken many of the thoughts on the next several pages from my 2016 book, *The Agile Web*. While I've modified them to fit the context of this book, and they serve as a very high-level overview, if you've read the earlier book, you may recognize some of the thoughts that follow.

There are three important milestones in the history of agile that we'll note here. For reference, everything that we'll be talking about came out of the Software Development Life Cycle (SDLC), which, as early as the 1960s, laid the groundwork for how many modern processes are performed, particularly software development. It has since been applied to marketing.

REQUIREMENTS

SYSTEM DESIGN

IMPLEMENTATION

TESTING

DEPLOYMENTS

MAINTENANCE

WATERFALL METHOD

First, there was waterfall

The waterfall methodology was first used in the early 1970s, after a decade of SDLC being the dominant methodology used in the software development community.

Although there are variations among the exact steps and names various people or companies use in the waterfall process, the general process is consistent. The central idea is that waterfall is a very linear process.

Changes during the latter phases of a waterfall project will often require major rework, and repetition of testing and other downstream activities.

In other words, if you get all the way to the "Implementation" step (the 3rd step in the chart above), and realize you missed something, or that you need to change the way something is currently created, it will require you to start from the beginning and re-integrate these new requirements, as well as a new design, and then to re-implement the code. With waterfall, it can be very costly and time-prohibitive to make changes, even if they massively improve the end product.

In addition, early computers were large, expensive, and almost impossible to obtain long amounts of time on. With a short amount of time to run your programs, you had to spend a lot of time making sure you got things right.

Introduction of Agile

What is agile?

> *"One should not first make the program and then prove its correctness, because then the requirement of providing the proof would only increase the poor programmer's burden. On the contrary: the programmer should let correctness proof and program grow hand in hand."*
> *Edsger W. Dijkstra, "The Humble Programmer," (1972)*

After decades the waterfall method, he availability of fast computing, the rise of the Internet, and the ubiquity of personal computers allowed more rapid development of software, and eventually web applications.

While several methodologies popped up earlier in the 1990s, including Rapid Application Development[17] (RAD), agile development was the most effective at "winning over" software developers.

In 2001, the Agile Manifesto[18] was born:

> "We are uncovering better ways of developing software by doing it and helping others do it. Through this work we have come to value: Individuals and interactions over processes and tools Working software over comprehensive documentation Customer collaboration over contract negotiation Responding to change over following a plan That is, while there is value in the items on the right, we value the items on the left more."

Agile centered around the belief in collaboration, iteration, and a more "social" (not to be read as "social media") approach to creating great products.

AGILE METHODOLOGY

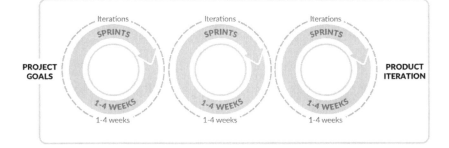

An agile software development "sprint" consists of several iterations over a period of days or weeks that is driven by product requirements.

Unlike the linear steps of the Waterfall methodology, the Agile methodology uses an iterative process to create products such as software. Through interactions that focus on specific goals and product features, called sprints, the product incrementally improves as it works against a product backlog that contains the features the end product must contain.

An agile project completes several such sprints throughout the project lifecycle, as opposed to a single development period in the waterfall method.

An agile project consists of multiple sprints that end in a new version of the product

Agile roles

There are 3 roles on an agile team:
- Product Owner
  - Plays a leadership role and represents the stakeholder's interests in returning ROI and

creating a successful product. Determines the goals and directions of the project and product and guides the team in its creation.

- Scrum Master
  - o Responsible for daily standup meetings as well as monitoring and tracking overall progress of the project. Works to make sure there are no blocks to the project's progress.
- Development Team
  - o Responsible for creating the product through a series of iterative sprints. Assign themselves tasks based on direction.

Within an agile project, all three of these roles are generally located within the same company or organization. It makes sense that everything from ownership of the product (or project) would take place from within the company in charge of the product or service.

We'll get back to these roles later in this book as we talk about agile brands and the evolution of the consumer-brand relationship.

Recap

Agile's rise and subsequent contributions to the world of software and the Web at large are wide-reaching and have changed the way we create and market products and services.

We'll talk next about how the agile methodology transitioned from a primary focus on technology and programming to an idea adopted in other process-centered areas such as marketing and product development.

7 | Agile Marketing & Design Thinking

"Agile marketing is the deliberate, long-term application of a specific Agile methodology to manage and improve the way a marketing team gets work done."
—Andrea Fryrear, The Agile Marketer

So where does all this talk about software development and writing code leave marketers? Despite increasing convergence between technology and marketing, there is more to it than that.

The agile approach can be applied to many things other than software development, including marketing, and branding.

Agile marketing

Agile marketing has come into prominence because of a number of recent advancements. We have seen a shift in preference to being more agile, and greater ability for marketers to become more agile because of:

- Big data's omnipresence in the marketing world, and our ability to get everything from real-time data to number-crunching for complex analysis more easily and cheaply.
- Dramatic decreases in data storage costs.
- Artificial intelligence which allows programmatic ad buying and other techniques that allow us to achieve decisions and results much quicker.
- Social media and other real-time or near-real-time communication tools that facilitate much quicker awareness and engagement (as well as the analysis of those occurrences).

While many factors have contributed, the points above certainly are part of what has paved the way. As more and more options become available for marketers to broadcast their messages, engage with consumers, and reach their key audiences, it becomes necessary to review, assess and optimize their efforts on an increasingly short timeline. This is where an agile approach shines.

How does agile marketing work?

"Agile marketing is a tactical marketing approach in which marketing teams collectively identify high value projects on which to focus their collective efforts. Teams use sprints (short, finite periods of intensive work) to complete those projects cooperatively."

What is Agile Marketing, and Why Should You Care? MarketerGizmo, Apr 20, 2015

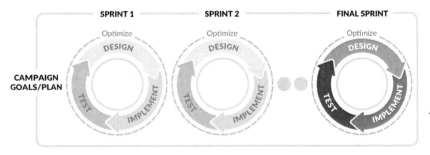

AGILE MARKETING

Agile marketing takes an incremental approach to achieving long-term marketing & campaign goals.

As you can see, our chart above now reflects marketing rather than *software development.* Overall, the steps don't change. Instead of planning our campaign out in detail at the beginning of the year or campaign, we now undertake sprints that bring monitoring and optimization along the way.

You may be thinking, "but I already do that." And in some ways, it's true. You place a programmatic media buy because you know that it will be optimized.

Some marketing methods lend themselves better to this approach, but you may also find that you are adopting more agile methodologies than you think.

The important thing is to keep monitoring and evaluations regular. There is simply no more "set and forget."

It's not enough to have a monthly or quarterly report that shows what happened. A report must be accompanied by analysis, evaluation and a list of what's going to happen next. There should always be a test going on to help you optimize something.

Why agile marketing?

"There's a refrain I've heard on every problem project I've run into. The developers come to me and say, 'the problem with this project is that the requirements are always changing.' The thing I find surprising about this situation is that anyone is surprised by it. In building business software requirements changes are the norm, the question is what we do about it."

—Martin Fowler, "The New Methodology"

The quote above from can easily be applied to marketing. We've moved beyond knowing exactly what we will be able to do in 12 months. Things change too rapidly, so we need a nimbler approach. As Fowler says, the requirements keep changing, and people are caught off guard when they should be planning for change and accounting for it in their strategies.

In a 2014 study, CMO's Agenda[19] found that over 60% of marketing leaders identified being agile as a high priority, yet only 40% rated themselves as agile. The study also found that marketers who identified as agile were 300% more likely to increase market share.

Our ability to measure everything we do as marketers has increased considerably and continues to grow as new platforms emerge and new methods of targeting are developed. The rise of big data from buzzword to multi-billion-dollar industry means that we are now inundated with so many metrics that we can't possibly report on them all. Big data has both good and bad effects on marketing and marketers.

Successful marketers filter out the noise and focus on the metrics that matter, not simply those that are easy to see. Those who adapt quickly to environmental changes will thrive[20]. By tapping into real-time and near real-time analytics and insights, and intelligently applying them to our marketing efforts, we can make the quicker decisions required in an agile process.

What about design thinking?

Agile has helped spawn methodologies that address business processes and broader scopes than software, websites, or digital marketing. One of these is "design thinking," which has its origins at IDEO, a design studio that does a lot of work in human-centered design and has completed a broad range of projects that involve user experience.

The easiest way to describe design thinking is as a philosophy that approaches business challenges with a clean slate. Instead of improving upon something which currently exists, it starts with the question, "What is the problem we're trying to solve?" and designs a solution from that.

Design thinking is similar to agile in that input is sought beyond the primary team doing the work, and it requires an iterative process to achieve the best solution to the problem.

What sets design thinking apart from agile is that it is even further from the waterfall methodology. Agile still assumes a particular end solution is the right approach. Design thinking does not make any such assumptions. The solution is designed around the *user* and not around a specific method, channel, or medium.

Agency agile, or how agile applies to business processes

Agile development, agile marketing, and even design thinking are applications of agile thinking to processes that fall outside software (or website) development. But what about higher-level business processes that go beyond how an individual project or tactic is approached?

This brings us to the agency agile approach, which while specifically designed for digital/marketing/advertising agencies, has applications for other types of businesses.

Patric Palm, CEO and Co-Founder, Favro, puts it this way[21]:

> *"One of these advantages is greater adaptability. More than anything, the evolution of client services in creative firms is driven by the need to accommodate project changes. In the new paradigm, project plans aren't written in stone; instead, every creative effort must be primed for constant adaptation. Agile accommodates this need for hyper adaptability by promoting workflows built around autonomous, yet aligned, teams, flexible planning, and experimentation. In an Agile workspace, agencies aren't tied down to an unbudging 'big idea.' And that's a good thing in an industry increasingly driven by uncertainty, where Monday's great project concept can become irrelevant or redundant by Tuesday."*

Recap

Originating from the widespread adoption of the agile method to produce software, agile marketing and design thinking are logical adaptations of this iterative methodology, applied to different types of business functions.

While "agile" alone is not a solution for every problem, its solution-oriented, iterative approach to problem solving has many applications at the strategic and tactical levels.

8 | The Agile Brand

"In military strategy, if you are unsure of the terrain ahead, then mobility is your key strategy. In volatile market conditions, branding is no different. Agility and responsiveness, adaptability and rapid reactivity are essential traits for market survival. Consequently, the brand strategy process must become faster, less linear, more flexible, and more collaborative."
—Daniel Matthews, Business 2 Community

Having discussed what *agile* is and means, let's talk more specifically about the current state of branding, and what I've defined as the Agile Brand.

Agility is built on principles of sprints and optimization discussed in the previous chapter, and on the fundamentals of branding.

There are five key things agile brands do which sets them apart:

1. Have an open dialogue with customers.
2. Tell stories that are genuine.
3. Use data to drive deeper insights and greater growth.
4. Think holistically about the customer experience.
5. Stay nimble by always listening.
6. Let go in order to have deeper relationships.

Have an open dialogue with customers

We all hear about engagement, but what does it really mean? To many digital marketers, it's a metric to be reported. Consumers rarely view engagement in the same way, or think of it all. In an era where advertising and marketing are so pervasive, customers aren't seeking engagement with brands. In fact, most people who do not work in the marketing world rarely, if ever, think about something like brand engagement.

Instead, customers want to *solve problems.* Some of these problems may be fairly trivial, such as wanting to laugh, or waste time while waiting for a plane. Some may be much heavier and important, such as wanting to improve their lives, take an important next step in their career, or start something new (a family, a business, a life transition). In seeking to solve these problems, customers seek *dialogue* with brands that can help them.

An estimated 70% of consumers have used social media for customer service, and companies are responding; 90% are forecasted to implement social customer service by 2020[22].

Since the advent of social media in the early 2000s, dialogue with customers has become increasingly important – but it brings potential risk. Customer service goes well beyond quickly solving a problem, now that the world can witness how well or poorly you treat your customers through social media.

Shep Hyken, best-selling author, says it well as he describes the very public aspect of customer service on social media, "When a customer posts a comment, good or bad, the world can see it.

They can also see how the company responds – if the company responds at all."

While open dialogue is not all about traditional customer service issues, that is certainly an important aspect. Thus, what brands often call "engagement" is really helping customers solve a challenge. Being an organization that is ready, willing, and able to engage in that dialogue is what separates an agile brand from the rest of the pack.

Tell stories that are genuine

We will explore this more in chapter 11, but any brand story must be authentic and stay true to your company values. It must also resonate with your customers' values and ideals. A cautionary tale shows why.

In the early 1990s, Oldsmobile needed brand revitalization. Its reputation was for making bland cars with little character, and no appeal to a younger buying demographic. In short, Oldsmobiles were for *old people*.

Oldsmobile's strategy was to show consumers that Oldsmobile was creating the *new generation* of their brand by bridging the gap between parents and children. They got celebrity parents including Ringo Starr and William Shatner to appear in advertisements, with the tagline "This is not your father's Oldsmobile" closing out each ad.

The result? While the cars were a little more modern than their predecessors, the ads managed to fall flat with the younger generation while alienating their core customer base, those *old* people that liked their Oldsmobiles just fine.

Zac Estrada says it well[23]:

> "Even for a '90s ad for a Cutlass Supreme, it's hopelessly corny. The long-term damage was said to be with the fact it alienated existing Oldsmobile buyers. Worst of all, it screamed that Olds was desperate to be cool again. And we saw how that turned out."

They got a former Beatle to help sell their product, for crying out loud. How could this go wrong?

Use data to drive deeper insights and greater growth

Many companies got on the "big data" bandwagon early, driving it on a path of growth that IDC predicts will reach in excess of $200 billion by 202024. Many realized that with big data came a lot of tough decisions about *which* data to look at, and *how* to sift through it all. Everything from financial and sales data, to website analytics, to real-time social media listening tools can clutter any database and reporting tool. This creates overload and confusion, often resulting in marketing and sales reports based on what data is easy to obtain and make sense of, rather than what data is valuable to understand.

Using data well means asking the right questions

It's way too expedient to pull a report based on easy numbers. Instead, agile brands understand that any great insights must come from asking the *right questions.* The somewhat obvious question I always come back to, when looking at a report, a chart, or any other gathering of metrics is this:

"What is the problem we're trying to solve?"

It's so ridiculously simple a question, yet it's amazing how infrequently it is asked. When a clear strategy is not readily apparent, taking the time to ask this gives us focus, and in the absence of focus we tend to think tactically based on the information which is most readily available.

When in doubt, rely on tried and true processes

I didn't always start out this way, but in several years of running a digital agency, I became a true believer in process. Not just process for process' sake, but good old-fashioned repeatable, measurable, scalable process.

While some creatives (as well as others) often bristle at the idea of too much process which might hinder innovation, I often use the following analogy to dispel this myth.

Consider ballroom dancing. You may not know a lot about it, but if you've ever seen a waltz, tango, or some other dance which requires fancy footwork, you've witnessed individuals who have a deep and fundamental understanding of where their feet need to be and when. I learned a bit about this when I filmed a documentary about ballroom dancing instruction a number of years ago.

Basic Box

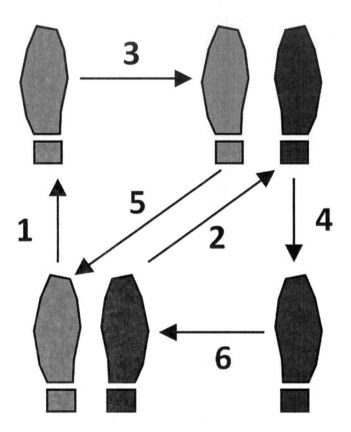

In ballroom dancing, when you know where your feet need to go, you can be truly creative. Image courtesy of Wikimedia Commons

I was impressed by the precision of the dancers, but even more by the fact that, despite 10 couples dancing the tango, each performance was different, and creative in its own right. What does this mean, exactly, you ask?

It means that when our feet know where to go, and we understand that "process" of what makes a waltz a waltz, we can then truly be creative, and *innovate.* Process helps eliminate clutter and confusion by providing constraints which allow great things to happen within an effective structure.

As a tried-and-true process, let's consider the scientific method that forms the basis of how most marketers have been practicing their craft since the profession began. With quicker and easier data available, it's easy to get distracted and short-change the process you learned back in school, but utilizing the cyclical structure of this tried-and-true method naturally complements an agile process.

Don't let the volume and ease of quantitative data outweigh qualitative insights

Big Data and increased access to insights based on number crunching (from a formerly intimidating array of sources and size of data sets) is now something that even small businesses can benefit from. But as you well know, there is are some things you can't glean from data!

Think holistically about the customer experience

As mentioned, consumers have become device-agnostic and want things when, where and how they prefer. The customer experience doesn't take place on one or two channels, nor does it always happen in real-time. With asynchronous communication platforms like Twitter and texting, customer service, sales, and social communication can happen anytime.

Let's go back to the diagram referenced as we talked about brands as relationships:

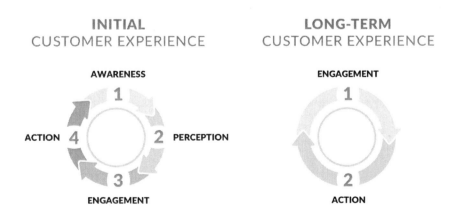

Our goal as marketers is to build our customers from the initial customer experience (on the left), into a continual state of engagement and action. While some may find this optimistic or perhaps unrealistic, if you have the right mix of customer need, engaging content, and the knack for understanding how to be a problem-solver with your customers, this is achievable. Keep in mind consumers' bandwidth, however. You can't reasonably expect constant engagement with them, but you can strive to be top of mind when they have the type of problem you are able to help them solve.

It is also critical to understand that this cyclical process is happening across devices, locations, and spans of days and months. The tools to put the story together are there, but you need to understand the wide variety of methods and places your customers are experiencing your brand.

Stay nimble by always listening

"The customer is always right" is a cliché we've all heard countless times. It's vital to *listen* to our customers so we can understand what they are saying, and why they *believe* they are right.

This process of listening and reacting has been made both easier and infinitely more complicated by the rise of social media, review sites, social media "influencers", and company websites that solicit feedback.

To be nimble and react to what your current and prospective customers say, what your competitors do, and what your critics write, you must be prepared to listen, analyze and adjust what you're doing at a moment's notice. So, keep in mind the point above about using data throughout your processes.

Nimble is both external and internal

One classic example of a brand being nimble is Oreo taking advantage of half the stadium going dark during the 2013 Super Bowl, by sharing their "you can still dunk in the dark" tweet. While it may have gotten a more enthusiastic response from digital marketers than the average consumer, it was a great example of a team agile enough to work outside a planned social media schedule and capitalize on a situation.

With the big game on pause for several minutes, not only did the Oreo team have time on their hands, so did consumers. The team managed to create messaging relevant to the Oreo brand. If there were months to prepare an advertisement around it, they might have come up with something more compelling, but the brilliance of the response was in its nimbleness, and a team that could react quickly while staying on brand.

Let go to have deeper relationships

Agile brands have a two-way relationship with their customers, particularly their *best* and *most loyal* ones. What does this mean?

First, let's revisit the three roles an agile project typically includes:

- Product Owner
- Scrum Master
- Development Team

Brand development and marketing still belong to the company doing the marketing. However, being agile means giving a little bit away in order to get more in return.

Dell's Ideastorm website, launched in 2007, gathers customer ideas for its products from customers through and gamifies the generation of ideas by showing "trending" suggestions, most recent ones, and other things that create a community around brainstorming for the company. Starbucks has done something similar in soliciting drink ideas from around the world. Roles such as generating new product ideas that are typically reserved for brand employees are now being outsourced to consumers.

I propose that the "product owner" role needs to be shared in a truly agile, successful brand. This does not mean giving up complete control, but once you open your brand up to an agile approach, you can't rigidly control elements like product development.

Further, it's important to realize that consumers *expect* this from you. It's not something that you can truly prevent. Consumers can now comment about you on social media, give reviews on Yelp, customize your products, and so much more.

There are certainly risks in this, but the benefits of embracing the new consumer role means that you can more easily incorporate their desires and preferences quickly in everything you do, thus delivering products that better meet their needs.

A few examples of agile brands

While there isn't a strict definition for an "agile brand," the attributes are easy to spot, including listening and responding to consumer needs and challenges while remaining true to their values. Changing messaging while staying true to their unique selling proposition and values has led many brands to success.

Domino's: changing the conversation

Why Domino's changed its messaging

"Mad Men's" Don Draper famously said, "If you don't like what people are saying about you, change the conversation." Domino's Pizza took a page from that playbook in 2010 when it changed its message and rebranded to Domino's without "Pizza" at the end.

Domino's had grown since its founding in Michigan in 1960, but its brand had become stale. It was perhaps best known for its "Avoid the Noid" campaign from the 1980s, and that recognition was doing little to boost sales with younger demographics.

The chain changed its messaging in 2010 just after its 50-year anniversary. Determined to change its reputation as a subpar pizza place, and change the conversation about Domino's, it scrapped its pizza recipe and started over with a new menu, and new name of simply Domino's.

The brand's advertising became all about challenging the status quo, even when that meant challenging itself as a company. It has managed to keep that messaging intact over the years, continually positioning itself as a game-changer and innovator, from enabling ordering via emojis to new and improved pizza recipes.

How it worked

From 2011 to 2016, Domino's stock grew by 700 percent, outperforming Papa John's (at only 300 percent growth). By challenging the status quo and taking responsibility for its own shortfalls, Domino's achieved extraordinary returns, while creating many happy customers and winning back prior defectors.

Starbucks: simplifying while expanding

Why Starbucks changed its messaging

Since its founding in Seattle in 1971, Starbucks' logo has evolved many times. It seemed to settle into a consistent design between 1987 and 2011 (with a brief misstep in 2008. Then, in 2011, the brand evolved not only its logo, but its messaging. Starbucks Coffee would now simply be known by its symbol logo, as the company name was taken out of the logo mark. The company also dropped "Coffee" from its name.

One obvious reason for the rebranding and revised messaging was Starbucks continuous expansion beyond "coffee" as it had grown internationally. Starbucks has expanded its food offerings, and introduced beer and wine in some markets. The messaging also evolved to involve customers more through cause-related initiatives and other programs.

Starbucks didn't set out to reinvent itself so much as to evolve and mature. The more sophisticated look has enabled the brand to grow and continue to expand around the world.

How it worked

Although there was some initial backlash against the new, simplified logo, Starbucks CEO Howard Schultz stood his ground,[25] unlike Tropicana and Gap, which rebranded during the same time frame – but backtracked in response to negative consumer reactions.

In the long run, Starbucks' simplified approach paid off. Schultz said, "The goal was not only to refresh the mark but to free the Siren from the ring, allowing her to be treated more artistically."

Just in case you were wondering how a fancy new logo and revised messaging correlated with increased revenues, between the years 2008 and 2014 (the rebrand occurred halfway through this period), Starbucks' stock price grew 948 percent. Yes, nearly 1,000 percent growth in a handful of years. While messaging wasn't the sole reason for that growth, the revised brand most certainly assisted!

Lowes Foods: question everything

Why Lowes changed its messaging

In 2014, North Carolina-based grocery chain Lowes Foods implemented a complete rebranding of everything from its logo to the layout of more than 100 stores in the Southeastern United States.

Faced with competition from other local and larger regional grocery chains, Lowes Foods failed to stand out. Martin Lindstrom, marketing guru behind Lowes Foods, told CNBC, "You can't compete on volume, you can't compete on prices because the online retailer will always win."

So instead of simply changing the logo, the company took a new approach from the ground up. It emphasized (instead of shied away from) the local aspect of the store. It added themed sections to stores (such as the Beer Den) that brought in a unique design and flavor to the grocery shopping experience. The agency that helped with the rebranding encouraged the retailer to follow in the steps of a theme park and not simply follow the lead of the next largest grocery store.

Most successfully, it implemented an element that was unique amongst its competitors: The Chicken Dance. Yes, that's right. When the latest batch of rotisserie chickens is finished cooking, the floor team plays and dances to the Chicken Song.

Originally created in the 1950s as the *duck* song (its original Swiss name is "Der Ententanz"), the Chicken song was reintroduced to the United States in the 1980s in Tulsa, Oklahoma[26] when an Oktoberfest group lacked duck outfits.

While it's been used before in advertising and promotions, Lowes was the first grocery store to incorporate this song into an experience within its retail environment.

How it worked

It's easy to call the Chicken Dance (you really must Google "Lowes Chicken Dance" for yourself) a silly gimmick, but it was part of a rebranding and rethinking of the grocery retailer's entire customer experience that resulted in a 23 percent increase[27] in transaction volume soon after the brand launch. The new brand works because it is cohesive and feels authentic to the setting and context of the stores.

It also works because of its strong focus on customer experience. Instead of competing solely on price, or even solely on appearances, the Lowes messaging engages customers in a personal, fun, and memorable way.

Lowes explains this by saying[28] "...our job is not to be an incrementally better grocery store. We want to create something different and unique in the grocery experience overall."

Recap

Being agile doesn't necessarily mean either evolutionary or revolutionary change. It all depends on the needs of the market, and the willingness of the organization to take risk.

What made both Starbucks and Lowes agile is their commitment to reinvention and taking risks, however big or small they might be perceived.

9 | The Agile Brand Manifesto

"The snake which cannot cast its skin has to die. As well the minds which are prevented from changing their opinions; they cease to be mind."
— *Friedrich Nietzsche*

As with the introduction of any concept, agile branding needs a clear statement that unequivocally defines what it is and describes the philosophy that guides it. Much as Agile Manifesto did that for programming, I'd like to do that for agile branding now.

I want to thank and give credit to the team who wrote the original Agile Manifesto for the inspiration. You can find all their names at AgileManifesto.org.

Through the evolution of brands from a simple visual indicator of ownership to their broad function today, we understand that a brand can be greater than the individual or individuals who created it, the teams who maintain it, and the products and services they represent.

Because of this, we have come to value the following:

- Long-term customers over short-term sales.
- Dialogue with customers over broadcasting one-way marketing messaging.
- Staying true to our values over doing whatever we can to generate profits.
- Continual improvement over maintaining the status quo.

While the constructs on the right remain important, we value those on the left more.

We also know that for a brand to be successful, it must open itself to consumers for feedback, ideas, and dialogue. No longer can brand decisions be made solely in a boardroom or by shareholders. Consumers want and need to feel a connection with brands in order for them to be truly successful.

The principles behind agile branding

To again mirror the efforts of the group who wrote the Agile Manifesto, I have compiled the principles that guide agile branding:

We follow these principles:

- Our highest priority is to add value to people's lives through meaningful interactions and tangible benefits that brands offer to customers.

- We believe brands play an important role in society, and when they are managed properly, they can add value to people's lives.

- We believe change can be a force for good and branding and marketing need to change to best serve their customers and society.

- We believe the future is bright and technology can be a force for good in the right hands and with the right motives.

- We believe that to make a great brand is to tie a core set of values to the products and services delivered.

- We also believe the world is in continual motion, and the ideas and thinking we currently share are subject to continual evolution as the practice of branding evolves.

Recap

We've now established a set of guidelines and principles we can follow to continue to foster the evolution of brands and maintain an agile approach to reaching and serving our customers.

10 | **The Duality of the Agile Brand**

"Brands are no longer based on the brand promise created by the organization – instead, it is the actions and experiences delivered to the customer. Brand reputation wins over brand promise every time."
—David Newberry, Brand Quarterly

Once when I was speaking on the topic of agile marketing at a conference, someone asked a question that should be addressed here: Doesn't it go ag*ainst the fundamentals of branding to be so agile, and adapt to change so easily? What about the core things that make up a brand?* For this reason, we need to think of the Agile Brand as being nuanced.

In Chapter 2, we described "timelessness" as one of the key aspects of a great brand. It's important to make sure we don't confuse matters. While much of our discussion of the agile brand has centered on creating a continually evolving entity, we should also be clear that there are certain brand elements which should not be readily modified.

Daniel Matthews[29] says the following:

> *"Today's brands must be flexible—evolving to meet rapidly changing consumer needs—but this doesn't mean a brand is infinitely malleable, or it would lose all meaning. Identify and preserve the core principle of the brand—the unalterable brand promise that the customer can rely on over time—while leaving all other facets in constant evolution."*

Thus, there are 2 components to an agile brand:

1. The things that don't change.
2. The things that do change.

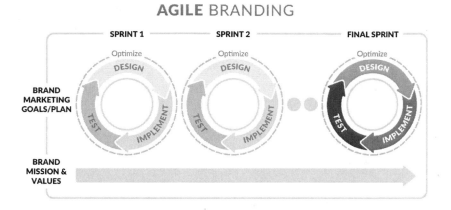

While your brand marketing and awareness efforts (top row) will inevitably change as you target new audiences, or as your current audiences evolve, your brand mission and values (bottom row) should remain relatively constant over time.

The things that don't (or seldom) change

Let's start with a deeper dive on the things that you should modify in your agile process. These include the elements that make your company stand the test of time.

Mission

Despite your need to reach audiences in new ways, introduce products and services, or even to rebrand, your mission shouldn't be subject to as frequent (or potentially as drastic) change. Changing your mission should be done carefully and it requires greater justification than a change in customer preference or marketing trends. After all, no matter what your logo looks like, your advertising says, or even who your target audience is, your company should always stay true to its purpose and reason for existence.

Take Facebook for example. Their mission since their beginnings in the early 2000s was always "To give people the power to share and make the world more open and connected." But in a letter published February 16, 2017[30], after a polarizing U.S. election, and much public discourse about bots and fake news, Facebook CEO Mark Zuckerberg expanded and further defined Facebook's mission beyond that shorter phrase to include more responsibility for building "social infrastructure," including the following phrase:

> *"Social media is a short-form medium where resonant messages get amplified many times. This rewards simplicity and discourages nuance. At its best, this focuses messages and exposes people to different ideas. At its worst, it oversimplifies important topics and pushes us towards extremes."*

As you can see, Facebook's overarching mission of giving people the power to connect didn't change completely, but based on larger events in the world, the mission of Facebook needed to be clarified and modified to take on challenges that were unforeseen as of its founding. It could also be said that this was a way of Facebook admitting that, while it maintains an altruistic bent in its mission, it is also a for-profit company that is intent on delivering returns to its shareholders. While you may not have such an extreme example of change in your market or business, there will undoubtedly be evolutions over time that may require changes or modifications to your mission.

Values

Corporate values have been in the spotlight for many reasons lately. A recent Nielsen poll[31] showed that over half (55%) of consumers would be willing to spend more on a product if the company that makes it shares their values. More importantly, this number increases to 70% when talking specifically about Millennials, who be the largest part of the workforce by 2020[32].

John Wooden, 12-year coach of the UCLA basketball team, and nicknamed the "Wizard of Westwood," said "The true test of a man's character is what he does when no one is watching." The same can be said for a company's values.

Values are what drives the company independent of profit margins, shareholder value, and other business key performance indicators (KPIs).

The important thing about corporate values to keep in mind is that to be perceived as genuine, and thus effective, they must remain constant. While different generations might have different ways of connecting with them, and companies may use ways of explaining them over time, what makes them ring true is their consistency and integrity.

Tony Hsieh of Zappos puts it this way:

> *"We believe that it's really important to come up with core values that you can commit to. And by commit, we mean that you're willing to hire and fire based on them. If you're willing to do that, then you're well on your way to building a company culture that is in line with the brand you want to build."*

It takes a lot of commitment to stand by your values no matter what. Would you, like Tony Hsieh, be willing to fire an employee because he or she violated your company values? Would you be willing to lose a customer because of them?

No matter what trends and fads come and go, your values define who you are, the types of people you represent, and the type of future you envision. Which is all great if your values are positive, inclusive, and do not come at someone else's expense.

But what about a company whose values include discrimination, exclusion, and inequality? The stance of Chik-fil-A against same-sex marriage in 2012 (before they half-heartedly walked it back a few years later), the Washington Redskins refusing to acknowledge there might be something amiss with their name (not the "Washington" part), or the NRA valuing the second amendment over logical discourse over firearms restrictions, are all examples of organizations whose values come at the expense of someone else.

We can often assume that the word "values" is a positive thing, but many different people (and shareholders) find value in different things. While this isn't a book about politics or civil liberties, it's important to note that a company's values *should* be something positive that inspires its employees, its customers, and the communities it serves.

So, while an organization shouldn't change its values on a whim, it needs to be cognizant of the responsibility it has to people everywhere, and the impact is has on the world.

The things that do change

Audience

There are two ways to look at how an audience changes over the life of a brand. First, you can look at audience shifts in terms of how an audience's preferences and behaviors change over time. This could be measured in everything from how they interact with your brand (e.g., a shift in mobile device usage, or increased adoption of social media for customer service) to their buying behaviors or other preferences.

The second way you can look at audience shifts is in how different audiences may find your products and services useful over time. You may go to market assuming that your product solves a specific audience's problems, but then find that you are instead being very successful with a completely different audience. What do you do? Depending on your strategic approach, you may decide to embrace this new audience, or you may shift your messaging and strategies to focus more on a different demographic.

Toyota's Scion brand is a perfect example of this phenomenon. Toyota launched Scion as a low-cost, highly customizable brand of uniquely designed cars in 2003, which came out of its internally-designated "Project Genesis" started in 1999[33] to design and market cars to millennials. As of 2014, there were five models from sporty to more utilitarian, and despite a heavy marketing focus on younger demographics, it failed to connect. Instead, Scion's models, and the boxy xB in particular, found a very different, and older, core audience, with Patrick George of Jalopnik[34] going so far as to say the models success was "because Scions like this second-generation xB were affordable and easy for arthritic retirees to get in and out of." Despite a very targeted Millennial marketing effort, Gen Xers and Baby boomers instead made up a significant portion of the brand's core customers, with some reporting the average age of a Scion customer was 49—far from the age of millennials.

Instead of embracing this and growing Scion in these segments, Toyota instead decided to shutter the brand on February 3, 2016, and fold its remaining successful car models into the parent brand[35]. Many say this was a missed opportunity. While the original audience didn't embrace Scions the way Toyota wished they would, the brand found a niche audience regardless.

The Scion xB found a very different audience (retirees) than Toyota had originally intended (millennials). Image courtesy of Wikimedia Commons.

Defining your audiences in terms of demographics can prove quite challenging, and often relies on assumptions that because people are the same age, or come from the same cultural background, they want the same things. This is not always the case. Take, for instance, Millennials, who have been called the most diverse generation in history[36].

This diversity makes it difficult for marketers to clearly define what *Millennials* are, what they like, how they act, and the types of products they want. While there are many generalities, such as their preference for supporting brands that clearly articulate their values (and whose values align with theirs), exactly what values a brand should have cannot be easily defined.

Because of this ambiguity, which will continue to increase with future generations, many marketers are moving away from targeting specific *demographic* audiences and moving toward targeting people at certain life moments. For example, two people of different ages and backgrounds who are both shopping for a new car loan for the first time actually have a lot in common.

Google has invested a lot of time and energy (and dollars) into this concept, which it dubbed "micro moments[37]" and separated into four primary categories:

- I-want-to-know moments.
- I-want-to-go moments.
- I-want-to-do moments.
- I-want-to-buy moments.

Thinking of audiences in terms of commonality of purpose as opposed to commonality of age, gender, culture, or generation affords marketers a very targeted way of looking at behavior and motivation.

Positioning

The Lowes Foods case study in chapter 8, demonstrated how a grocery chain was able to change its positioning, from a "typical" retailer which couldn't be distinguished from any number of competitors, into one that has a unique voice, character, and positioning as an alternative brand that takes pride in its food, ingredients, and process. Despite this change in branding and positioning, nothing changed about Lowes' commitment to quality or the other values it has adhered to since its founding.

Strategies & tactics

Finally, the strategies used to tie your business goals to your audiences, and the methods used to position your organization and its products and services will most definitely change over time. And, for an agile brand, these things will be modified regularly.

Just think about the strategies that Coca-Cola uses now versus 45 years ago. Even 20 years ago, the Web was in its infancy, and hardly the place to sell soft drinks. When the 1971 commercial featuring "I'd Like to Teach the World to Sing" aired, no one could have predicted that 45 years later, Coca-Cola would have a 55-person North American Social Centre[38] functioning as a real-time newsroom and social media marketing war room. While that is an obvious example because the medium (social media) simply didn't exist before this millennium, there are plenty of times that strategies and tactics have changed without changing the medium used.

Other Things to Consider

Let's end the chapter with a few additional things to keep in mind.

Unique selling proposition

Somewhere in between your values, which should never change, and your positioning, which may fluctuate with changing times and audience preferences, your unique selling proposition should not be lightly tossed aside, yet it may change relative to how some of the factors above ebb and flow over time.

Competition

Another constantly changing dynamic is the competitive landscape. Many companies have seen new and more disruptive competition from longstanding rivals as well as newer upstart companies with new and novel business models.

Think about how Amazon has disrupted the brick-and-mortar retail industry, how Uber has disrupted transportation, or how Stripe, Venmo and other "fintech" or financial technology companies are disrupting more traditional banking, payment, and credit services.

Recap

Understanding the duality of the agile brand will help you keep differentiating between the constants to which you must stay true, and the ever-changing factors that keep marketers, CEOs, and everyone else at a company on their toes.

11 | How to Create an Agile Brand

"...Being multidimensional beats being single-minded. Surprise beats consistency. Share of emotion beats share of mind. The best... brands have always understood this instinctively."
—Brian Millar, Emotional Intelligence Agency

There are six principles that I believe are critical to being a successful agile brand:

- Understand that change is the only constant.
- Identify when evolutionary vs. revolutionary approaches are needed.
- Make adaptivity and collaboration part of your culture.
- Stay true to your values no matter what.

- Keep in mind that It's not about channels and mediums, it's about customer experience.
- Listen *to*, don't talk *at.*

Understand that change is the only constant

While it seems that it's only in the age of technology that everyone complains about being too busy and things moving too quickly, this isn't the case. As early as 500 BC, Heroclitus said "the only thing that is constant is change."

You need to find ways to take advantage of change, and use it for your advantage.

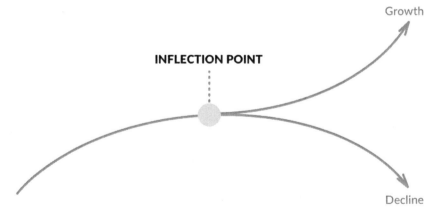

In differential calculus, an inflection point is a point on a curve at which the direction of the curve changes. As illustrated above, this can point to a downward or upward trajectory, but the inflection point is the place at which that change happens.

In business, an inflection point is the point at which something changes in a company or organization for the better or worse.

Maintaining the status quo (trying to stay on the same trajectory) for too long is not only bad for business, but it's also impossible in a world where disruption occurs so frequently. Agile brands understand that it is of continual importance to find new inflection points.

How exactly does a brand do that, you ask? By listening, monitoring, and having methods and means to understand when things are changing and the combination of tools and talent to understand what to do next.

Identify when evolutionary vs. revolutionary approaches are needed

The Starbucks and Lowes case studies provide examples that contrast with one another in terms of the degree to which change was required and implemented. Starbucks took a more evolutionary approach and continues to evolve to this day. Slowly evolving its logo design to be more inclusive of its product offerings and focus, Starbucks has continued steady change to keep pace with its customers and maintain a growing, profitable corporation.

Lowes Foods, on the other hand, was at a point where it needed to grow or continue to decline. Lowes understood that it needed a *revolutionary* approach to its brand in order to maintain relevance and compete in a changing marketplace.

Just as in these examples, you need to know when to take which approach for your own brand. You may need to take each of these tacks at different times. Generally speaking, you don't want to continually take a revolutionary approach because you run the risk of alienating loyal customers. They may follow you through one reinvention, but too drastic change too often may not inspire the loyalty which is also critical to a successful brand

Make adaptability and collaboration part of your Culture

It's also not enough to just be adaptive. Without a culture and processes for easy collaboration both internally and with external partners, being truly agile will not be possible.

It's not about channels and media, it's about customer experience

We need to stop thinking only in terms of the individual channels we reach customers through. Instead, we have to think of our customers in terms of their overall experience with our brand.

As noted, customers are becoming more and more "device agnostic" and you could even say they are "channel agnostic" as well. Whether they choose to visit a store, or shop on their phone, text, tweet or even make a good old-fashioned phone call depends on many external factors brands can't anticipate.

To combat this, we must make our communications, marketing, commerce and customer service agile and channel agnostic as well. This is what creates a great customer experience.

Listen *to*, don't talk *at*

To create a holistic customer experience, it's important to use those channels as a means of two-way communication, rather than to deliver one-way messaging directed *at* consumers.

Instead, engage in a dialogue with your customers, and even if you're not actively communicating with them, listen to what they have to say.

As I've often told potential and current clients who were reluctant to fully engage or participate in social media, people are talking about you whether you are present on the platform or not.

Not having a Facebook page doesn't prevent people from disparaging your products on that network. Not to say that they are always talking about you in a negative way, either. But regardless of whether it is good, bad, or a mix, it is important that you hear and understand the conversation around your brand.

Recap

An agile brand requires listening, conversation, and responsiveness to your customers, and the tools available today make this both easier to start, yet more daunting a task to do well because of the wealth of information (useful or less useful) available due to the advent of Big Data.

Unlike the early days of advertising and marketing, where real-time data and analytics were simply not available en masse (only in focus groups or smaller studies), successful companies today understand that their brands can more easily and (with the assumption that both a great volume of data and more accurate data is more readily available today than in the past) more *accurately,* be shaped by the consumers who use their products. In addition, the most vocal brand advocates often want to feel that they have a special connection with that company. Encouraging this mutual relationship provides this open door for people to love your brand and share it with others.

12 | An Agile Brand Example

"Agile brands are nimble to risk and quick to seize opportunity. They aren't afraid to let go of the consistency handcuffs or bend rules when necessary."
—Thomas Ordahl, Landor from Forbes.com

While there are many great examples of brands that have been able to adopt an agile approach to their brand and marketing, we'll focus on one that has worked through several types of change over the last several years.

Case study: Netflix embraces an agile approach

Netflix, founded in 1997, has transformed its business model three times since inception. Its business model, however, was disruptive at its start and then experienced several disruptions itself.

Netflix logo from 1997-2000

Iteration 1: mail order

The story goes that Netflix co-founder Reed Hastings was fed up after a $40 late fee from Blockbuster for renting *Apollo 13*, and started the company to prevent anyone else from enduring the same experience. That story is not exactly true[39], but made up to illustrate one of the problems that the upstart Netflix was trying to solve.

Originally, Netflix was a solely mail-order DVD rental service, competing with the lucrative brick-and-mortar video rental business. In 1997, Blockbuster was by far the dominant video rental player. Having just been bought by Viacom for $4 billion in 1994[40], it appeared that there was no end in sight for the video rental market.

Netflix logo from 2000-2014

Iteration 2: streaming added

When Netflix started in the late 1990s, no one could predict that streaming movies and TV shows over the Internet would become a disruptive business model. After all, with limited dial-up speeds, studio concerns over digital copying and rights management, and lack of standardization for Internet video file formats, the decline of physical retail video outlets was not easy to foresee.

In 2007, Netflix began streaming TV shows and movies, taking advantage of higher Internet bandwidth and a mindset that embraced digital media platforms (such as iTunes) versus purchasing DVDs and VHS. Hulu, a joint venture with Disney, 21st Century Fox, Comcast and Time Warner, was launched the same year and upped the competition for streaming TV shows almost instantly. Another competitor, Redbox, which focused on the physical DVD market, was also a strong player in 2007, surpassing Blockbuster in locations[41], and providing stiff competition for Netflix.

By 2010, while Netflix was expanding its streaming services to places like Canada (underscoring the shift in Internet usage), Blockbuster was filing for bankruptcy[42].

Which brings us to the "New Coke" move of Netflix's history. In April 1985, at the height of Pepsi's popularity, Coca-Cola changed its formula to compete with its sweeter-tasting rival, introducing New Coke. An immediate public backlash resulted and led to the introduction of "Classic Coke" which was simply the original recipe people had enjoyed for decades. While Coca-Cola eventually recovered from its misstep, it cost the company a lot of money and the new product was ultimately discarded.

Netflix, in an attempt to differentiate its streaming and mail order businesses, announced on September 18, 2011[43] that it would split the two services. A new company called Qwikster would handle the DVD business and add video games, while Netflix would retain the streaming side of things. The company also announced a price increase.

Qwikster logo, for the would-be Netflix spinoff that would never be

Public sentiment showed itself rapidly, in one of the first major demonstrations of public outrage at rebranding in the social media age. Perhaps only The Gap's rebranding roughly a year prior received such a negative response. What had seemed like practical and logical business decision set off a tidal wave of anti-Netflix sentiment that demonstrated that consumers felt betrayed by a brand they had come to love. According to

Huffington Post's assessment of sentiment on social media, negative messages were overwhelmingly in the majority[44], as illustrated below:

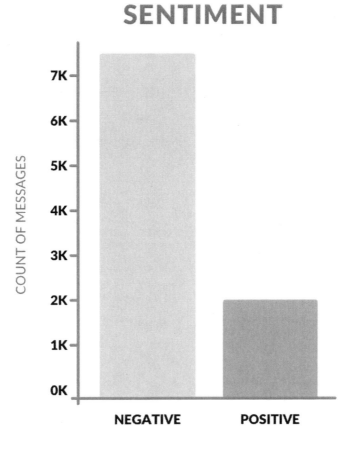

Huffington Post's analysis of social media sentiment using the tool Viral Heat, circa September 21, 2011

The quantifiable impact of this announcement and decision are staggering. In its third quarter announcement, Netflix reported losing 800,000 subscribers, and its stock fell nearly 30%[45].

What went wrong? In this modern era of consumer-brand relationships, making major changes is a difficult proposition. While the numbers the Netflix board of directors were undoubtedly looking at favored this approach from a revenue and profitability perspective, they failed to take into account the most important aspect of their business: the customer.

Or, as Nick Wingfield and Brian Stelter put it in the New York Times:

> *"Like many other companies built in Silicon Valley, Netflix prides itself on its analytical, data-driven approach to making decisions. But it made a classic business misstep. In its reliance on data and long-term strategy, the company underestimated the unquantifiable emotions of subscribers who still want those little red envelopes, even if they forget to ever watch the DVDs inside."*

Less than a month later, on October 11, 2011[46], Netflix reversed its decision to split off Qwikster, and, despite keeping the rate increase intact for subscriptions, public outrage died down.

After an apology from CEO Reed Hastings, and a shift back to business as usual, Netflix ended up with a profitable year. As time went by, however, new challenges arose. With traditional video rental dead, and streaming services proven as a viable business model, several competitors including Hulu were coming to market.

In addition, Netflix was having increasing difficulty negotiating with the original content providers it relied on for programming. From a customer perspective, who cared how easy it was to stream content on Netflix if they couldn't find anything they liked? This was the impetus for the next iteration of the Netflix brand.

Netflix logo, June 2014-present

Iteration 3: focus on original content

To combat the onslaught of streaming competitors and continual challenge of licensing and access to the programming subscribers wanted, Netflix would need to take another step in its evolution.

Its first original show was "House of Cards," which premiered February 1, 2013, and ushered in the era of Netflix becoming a source of great content unavailable anywhere else. By the end of 2016, Netflix had 30 original shows available or in development[47], and Chief Creative Officer Ted Sarandos claimed their original content budget would grow beyond its current $6 billion in 2017[48]. As of April 2017, there were 60 original feature films on Netflix, in addition to all the shows.

The risk and cost of relying on other people's content became too great. While Netflix still has plenty of third-party movies and shows, because it has diversified and established itself as an original channel and content producer, it can better weather any licensing deals that end.

What are the lessons?

Clearly, having entered the market as a disrupter, and then weathered several disruptions to its own business, Netflix qualifies as an agile brand. Let's figure out what we can learn from this example.

Lesson 1: embrace disruption

Netflix started as a disruptor. There was no reason to believe that Blockbuster or its many smaller rivals could be unseated from their video rental position of strength.

Despite this, Netflix focused on what it needed to do best: make people's lives easier (i.e., avoid having to go to the video store), and provide them the content they wanted to watch. This sharp focus on solving problems led to its quick rise in popularity and adoption, and the strong positive feelings that customers had for the service.

Agile brands need to keep this lesson in mind. If you are not actively working to solve a problem for your customers, they are not going to feel loyalty toward you. Relationships exist because of a give and take, but if consumers feel like they are giving more than they're getting, they will quickly find alternatives.

Lesson 2: embrace evolution

Netflix today looks very different from the company we were introduced to at the end of the 20th century. While its logo alone has changed twice since its introduction, the bigger changes come from how it has been able to adapt to external forces and thrive as it does.

Starting out in the mail order business, Netflix had to convince consumers to wait for the mail instead of driving to their favorite video store. But it turns out that the timing was right. Widespread Internet adoption allowed people to browse and search for titles from home, That, combined with growing dissatisfaction with video rental company practices (such as late fees), helped form the perfect environment for Netflix to thrive.

Next came the challenge of the changing nature of consumers' relationship to media. While the mail order business was lucrative, the growth of the Internet was hard to ignore, and Netflix was wise to adopt streaming early.

Finally, continued pressure to offer the best content to its audiences led Netflix to become a content creator in addition to providing access to others' content. This helped cement its importance in the entertainment industry, so that even if every production studio pulled their content from Netflix, it could technically still stand on its own based on original programming. Deciding to focus on investing in and creating great quality content helped it stand out from the competition.

The secret to agility is always being willing to adapt and change as long as your core values remain intact. The value of Netflix was always in making access to great entertainment easy. The delivery mechanism and even the entertainment itself changed over the years, but the promise always remained the same.

Lesson 3: learn from your mistakes

Clearly the Qwikster premise was a misstep, and Netflix was wise to change its approach after the ensuing public outrage. While it must have looked good from a numbers perspective, forcing its customers to deal with both a rate increase and two accounts with two different services was too much for them.

This example underscores the importance of understanding both data and those unquantifiable elements of your customer relationship; both must be taken into account. There isn't a single metric that you can use to guide your decisions.

It's also important to note that Netflix listened to its customers, which is so critical. While those three weeks before Netflix retracted its decision to split into two businesses seemed to last forever, in the pre-social media era of the mid-1980's, it took Coca-Cola three months to reverse its New Coke decision and bring back the original formula[49].

Even though the original decision was based on listening to the metrics and analytics that pointed to greater profitability, the ultimate reversal resulted from listening to customer sentiment and comments. The consumer eventually won, and Netflix was able to recover.

Lesson 4: don't be afraid to take a risk

Finally, beyond all of its other challenges, the ultimate key to Netflix' success was to give its customers what they wanted: great programming to watch. Remember as well that this decision was made 16 years after the company was founded. Many companies do not act so boldly and are not willing to make such large changes and investments nearly two decades into their history.

This became an increasing challenge as other content producers began to see Netflix as a threat rather than a distribution channel. As a content channel with no original content of its own, Netflix would always be vulnerable to the latest contract negotiation or threat to pull movies or shows. But as a content producer of great original programming that could only be accessed via a Netflix subscription, the tables turned.

With a focus on creating great original programming, Netflix ensured it would not be as vulnerable to external threats, and this ability to adapt yet again helped the company fend off challenges from myriad rivals.

Recap

Netflix is a great example of an agile brand because it went from a disruptor to surviving as a company that was on the verge of being disrupted several times. In addition, it was able to recover from consumer backlash over its Qwikster decision, which many companies don't survive. Finally, it adapted yet again by becoming a major producer of original content.

Staying true to its promise to deliver great content quickly and easily to its customers meant that Netflix was able to adapt to meet this need by creatively solving several challenges as they presented themselves.

Part 3
Building a Successful Agile Brand

13 | Storytelling and Agile Brands

"If you don't give the market the story to talk about, they'll define your brand's story for you."
—David Brier

As branding has been evolving, the need for brands to tell unique and authentic stories that portray their mission and values has grown continually stronger.

Jay Baer, author and founder of *Convince and Convert*, says, "If your stories are all about your products and services, that's not storytelling. It's a brochure. Give yourself permission to make the story bigger."

How to tell a story with your brand

An obvious place to tell your organization's story is on the "about" or "history" section of your website or marketing collateral. But the most effective brand storytelling occurs organically throughout everything you do.

The fundamentals of brand storytelling are the fundamentals of storytelling in general. Here are a few ways to tell a great story with your brand:

- Make it educational.
- Make it authentic.
- Make it relatable.
- Make it shareable.

Let's explore these in a little more depth:

Make it educational

Think about the last time a friend or colleague told you about a brand or product they like. Chances are, one of the things that stood out was something they *learned* while reading about the product, reading its history, or maybe even using the product.

People like to share something new or unexpected about brands they love with their friends, family and colleagues. Giving them something they can use to teach others motivates them to embrace and remember the information. In the act of teaching someone else, they also build greater affinity for your brand or product.

Make it authentic

It's time to stop thinking in the broadcast mode of marketing. Simply *saying* something isn't enough. Claiming to be the best, the fastest, or the friendliest means nothing without proof, and proof isn't just statistics, but meaningful interactions that build relationships.

This isn't just a nice idea, it's something that consumers are demanding. A recent global survey by Cohn & Wolfe[50] found that a large majority (87%) of consumers felt it was important for brands to "act with integrity at all times." This is even more impressive when you take into account that the survey participants ranked authenticity above innovation (72%) and product uniqueness (71%) when asked what they valued most in a brand.

It's also time to stop taking obvious actions that can easily be read as plays at being genuine. Or, as Jill Byron said in a recent article in *Advertising Age*[51], "Don't say you are authentic—be authentic."

Let's take it a step further, though. As brands have moved beyond the realm of ideas, and into experiences and relationships, being the best means *proving* that continually over time. Authenticity is not established overnight. It takes a long-term commitment to staying true to a set of values and acting on them.

Make it relatable

The best way to make your brand's story memorable is to relate it to your audience. What is challenging in this is that, in a continually changing world, any of the following may be true:

- Your audience's tastes change over time.
- You are appealing to multiple audiences, often with different values.
- Your company is going through transformation whether through acquisitions or changes in the market.
- Your products or services are evolving over time.

With all of the changes, different focus areas, and competing or conflicting tastes, you have your work cut out for you. Fortunately, by focusing on the essence of what makes your brand unique you can cut through the clutter and find a way to relate to your audiences. You may be able to filter your brand's values through a slightly different lens for each audience.

To be relatable means that you appeal to someone's sense of values, and that you solve a problem for them. Appealing to values has become a very important focus for most brands, which do everything from engaging in corporate social responsibility (CSR) campaigns, to encouraging employee volunteering.

Brands that truly solve their customer's challenges find ways to relate to them by understanding what the customer needs to accomplish to be satisfied.

Solving a challenge could be as simple as making them laugh (who doesn't need a little humor in their life?), but when someone truly relates to a brand, it's because that brand addressed a need. When a brand tells its story, it should incorporate a relatable challenge that they've addressed.

Make it shareable

What good is a story no one remembers, or isn't easy for your customers, fans, and employees to tell? While it may not be as obvious as the first two points, having a story that is easy to share is every bit as important.

Think of aspects of great stories that you could leverage for your own brand. A hero overcoming adversity, an unexpected or unique twist, or perhaps some element that is especially relevant to or resonates with your core audience.

While an effective story arc (beginning, middle and end) is important, it's not enough. The story needs to resonate enough with both the teller and the listener. For example, it isn't beneficial if you have a story that could be compelling, if it can't be embraced by the storyteller to drive the point home.

Just as importantly, making your brand more educational, relatable, and authentic in everything you do ends up making it more shareable as well.

Case Study: Eataly and the art of storytelling:

Eataly in Hamburg, Germany. Image Courtesy Wikimedia Commons.

Take for example Eataly, a brand that started in Italy, but was imported to the United States by Mario Batali and Joe Bastianich in 2012. Everything about the Eataly experience is built around educating the consumer with the goal of empowering them to tell their Eataly story to others. The Eataly website says it all:

"Eataly is MORE than a supermarket with restaurants. Our signs will give you the story behind every product we sell and serve, illuminating the vignettes that make Italian food culture so full of personality and warmth."

When you walk into an Eataly location, you are immersed in all things Italian food and cooking. To someone like me who doesn't do a whole lot of cooking, this could be slightly intimidating. But instead of overwhelming with a lot of options, Eataly takes a strong stance on educating the consumer.

This translates into everything from signage which explains the origins of ingredients, recipes, and other background information, to the way food servers always share the background of the food being served. While much of it is directly beneficial to someone purchasing food or groceries at an Eataly location, some of it serves to give the customer "insider" knowledge, building an affinity which allows the customer to be a greater part of the experience.

In their research-based case study of Eataly, Francesca Montagnini and Roberta Sebastiani[52] discuss the changing role of retail and how it's not enough to simply offer goods and services at a fair price:

"Customers are changing their desires and expectations, seeking for more variety and customization than they used to in the past. The attention shifts from the material product and service to the sharing of knowledge, typical of the post-modern era, transforming consumption into an immaterial process where the transmission of symbolic meanings exercises a determinant role in respect to the product/service itself."

So how does Eataly apply the concepts we talked about above?

Make it educational

This one is easy. Everything at Eataly is centered around the idea that an educated customer is a good customer. Through signage and a well-trained staff, they reinforce this throughout the customer experience.

Make it authentic

Part of Eataly's value is its ties to Italian heritage and culture. In its American stores, there is a strong emphasis on the food's history and authenticity. The stories that describe how and why food is prepared a specific way involve authentic storytelling about where these traditions originated.

Make it relatable

Eataly educates and informs customers through a friendly, sometimes humorous approach to explaining things. You are never meant to feel excluded or that you should already know what you're doing in order to walk into an Eataly location. Instead, from the moment you arrive, you're surrounded by educational help, whether printed items or staff trained to be helpful.

Make it shareable

By sharing all of the information it does, Eataly creates an army of informed consumers who now have "insider" knowledge about Italian food and cooking. These educated customers can't help but pass this on to the people they cook for, share meals with, or discuss culinary topics with. By giving its customers an edge with this background information, Eataly becomes a valuable source of information, and their stories, ideas and messages get shared again and again.

Recap

By telling a story, and finding ways to draw your audiences into it, you can build a stronger relationship. But a story alone isn't enough. It must come from a genuine place that connects not only with your brand's values, but with your audience's. It needs to be something that both your employees and your customers can tell and want to tell others about.

The benefits of a message that is easy to share means your story can take on a life of its own and allow your customers to feel they are a part of that story. That is a win-win.

14 | The Agile Brand's Responsibility to Society

If people believe they share values with a company, they will stay loyal to the brand.
—Howard Schultz, CEO, Starbucks

I feel it's important to address one other key aspect of brands that is part of the "new normal." It's not enough to simply make a great product, or offer an amazing service. It's also not enough to simply engage with our audiences on a regular basis. There needs to be something more, and truly successful brands have tapped into this.

Just as an agile brand must establish a bi-directional relationship with individual consumers to be successful, there must also be a symbiotic relationship with the world at large. This can play out in ways that impact society, the environment, or other areas that have a large cultural impact.

According to McKinsey[53], while many corporations were initially skeptical about the benefits of a strong corporate social responsibility (CSR) program, many have now integrated them so fully into their operations that they are able to see tangible benefits.

While the public at large expects more of brands now, a Nielsen survey[54] showed that 73% of Millennials are willing to spend more on a product if the brand supporting it adheres to sustainable values. To add to that, four in five Millennials expect their favorite companies to publicly state their corporate citizenship philosophy and activities.

Internal culture and the future of brands

We've spent most of this book talking about external communications, and how brands communicate with consumers.

But very important brand components, especially as brand values grow increasingly important to consumers, are companies' internal cultures, the work ethics they promote, and how they treat their employees.

Thom Wyatt, Managing Director of Siegel+Gale, a global brand strategy firm, puts it this way[55]:

> *"With the U.S. unemployment rate now at its lowest level in the post-recession era, the war for talent has intensified. In 2017, as work increasingly becomes a part of a person's identity, the role of a company brand will be a powerful differentiator for attracting talent. For potential recruits, the brand reputation that matters is company culture. Millennials are now the dominant generation in the workplace, and they ask questions about diversity, ethics, and the meaningful outcomes the company seeks to create in the world. For today's engaged employees, it's not enough to create great products and enjoy strong business results; they want to see diversity stats, social responsibility metrics, and the purpose and values that provide the cultural glue for a workforce."*

Let's a look at Uber as a recent example. With countless reports of rampant sexism, and a generally toxic corporate culture, by mid-2017 the company was in crisis. On June 6, 2017[56], 20 employees were fired after 215 reports of discrimination, unprofessional behavior and bullying, and sexual harassment were being actively investigated.

A few days later, Uber CEO Travis Kalanick, and Board Member David Bonderman resigned[57], and a few weeks later in September 2017, Uber was banned in London, with the claim it was not a "fit and proper" private car-hire operator and references to several aspects of the company that needed to be improved in order to be reconsidered.

This prompted an apology[58] from Uber's new CEO, Dara Khosrowshahi, which Uber said was a step in the right direction, and made one thing obvious: the ban in London had everything to do with Uber's culture. While it wasn't solely about a culture of sexism (there are other issues we don't have time to go into here), that toxic culture cost Uber the ability to operate in the third largest city in Europe[59].

So, how's that for a strong relationship between a brand and its internal culture?

Beyond company culture

Positive company culture is a major attribute when potential employees are looking for jobs, but the impact extends beyond that.

Much is written about company culture and its importance to the way a brand reflects on the outside world. For instance, the toxic workplaces of some Silicon Valley startups, including Uber, have had a negative effect on both consumer perceptions and their bottom lines. In other words, culture can have either very positive or very negative effects.

Agile brands should think about company culture as a differentiator. David Cummings, Co-Founder of Pardot, describes it this way:

> *"Corporate culture is the only sustainable competitive advantage that is completely within the control of the entrepreneur."*

In other words, company culture is not simply a bullet point on your careers page. It's something that consumers are interested in, and that can help (or hurt) you in the marketplace.

In a recent study of Millennial professionals by Eleventy Group[60], 70 percent said that a company's corporate social responsibility program would influence their interest in working for an employer. That says a lot about how important it is that employers embrace their values and provide opportunities for employees to participate in helping good causes.

A brand's overarching role in society is where corporate values come into play in a very real way, and that role extends a company's overall responsibility beyond t its fiduciary responsibility to shareholders. While a corporate social responsibility program is a formal way for a company to realize its values, there need to be other ways that company values can play out.

Recap

Social responsibility must be more than a marketing ploy to reach Millennials because it's something they care about. Instead, it must be translated into everything the company does. Consumers in general (not just Millennials,) want to feel good about the choices they make and the dollars they spend.

The agile brand understands this, and incorporates this thinking throughout everything it does instead of simply choosing words that sound good on its marketing materials. Social responsibility is becoming a prerequisite for being competitive as a business. Agile brands understand that their values matter, and must be genuinely expressed and demonstrated.

15 | Agile Brands and Future Generations

"Mass advertising can help build brands, but authenticity is what makes them last. If people believe they share values with a company, they will stay loyal to the brand."
—Howard Schultz, CEO, Starbucks

Just as past generations had their own unique relationship to brands, this dynamic will continue to evolve over time. Let's take a look at a few aspects of branding as they relate to the generations which will shape our economy and society over the decades to come.

Millennials

At this point, Millennials aren't a "future generation" but much of the current and near future workforce, and they will comprise much of the consumer base that brands will focus on for years to come. While targeting solely on generational demographics is becoming less favored as we discussed in previous chapters, the overall ideals, behaviors and preferences expressed by Millennials are still an influence on the market.

This generation might very well be the last one for which there is such a focus on the *generation* itself, as we'll discuss a little bit later on in this chapter.

The millennial generation has had a substantial influence on how brands approach consumer engagement and relationships, and in my opinion, this has generally been for the better. This also means that brands that have failed to be sufficiently responsive to the needs of this generation, which is the largest generation to come along in a while, will struggle to stay relevant.

Sebastian Buck writes in *Fast Company*[61]:
"Young people are making brand choices—some of which will last a lifetime—in an era of dramatic political and cultural events. Those brands that stand in accordance with young

people's values will be more likely to "win the future" than those that do not fully understand them or ignore them out of risk aversion or ambivalence."

According to the Enso World Value index[62], brands such as Proctor & Gamble, Newman's Own, and AAA have great brand recognition and favorability with baby boomers, but do not perform nearly as well with the Millennial generation, which prefers brands like Starbucks, Kickstarter, and H&M.

Stop and think about that for a minute. When you compare Newman's Own's branding efforts with Starbucks, what are the differences? Even though the former makes a strong stance about donating all profits to charities, Starbucks has captured the Millennial generation's mindshare because it has found ways, despite being a very profitable corporation, to put its values and efforts to help causes front and center. In this comparison, it's not a matter of one company doing more or being better than the other, it's a matter of the visibility of those efforts.

In order for brands to be successful with Millennials, they need to be genuine in their efforts to support causes which promote their values, but they also need to find ways to make these efforts visible in a way that this generation values. Brands also need to find ways to allow consumers to meaningfully interact with them. Things such as soliciting ideas and feedback openly about products and customer service make the interaction between brands and consumers more natural.

To go back to our comparison, think about how Starbucks solicits drink ideas from its customers, how it uses mobile apps, and many other tools and channels that engage and encourage an ongoing dialogue. This is the type of relationship that agile brands need to maintain in order to stay relevant.

Gen Z

This brings us to Gen Z, made up of those born after 2004[63], and who will, comprise nearly 40% of all consumers by 2020[64]. This generation is even more interested in social activism than the Millennial generation, according to research, and has gotten quite a bit of attention for that.

While Gen Z has been incorrectly labeled as having a short attention span, research has pointed to something interesting instead. Gen Z has developed what has been referred to as an "8-second filter", or the ability to quickly make decisions about how to narrow their choices.

Jeremy Finch puts it this way in a *Fast Company* article:

> *"They've grown up in a world where their options are limitless but their time is not. As such, Gen Z have adapted to quickly sorting through and assessing enormous amounts of information... Once something has demonstrated attention-worthiness, Gen Z can become intensely committed and focused. They've come of age with an Internet that's allowed them to go deep on any topic of their choosing and learn from like-minded fans."*

This means a few things for brands and marketers. First, long-form content marketing it isn't dead, but we need to find a way to get younger consumers in the door first, so to speak. Second, now more than ever, we need ways to present ourselves as unique and valuable in a shorter and shorter time frame.

As marketing movements such as the one focused on "life moments" over generational marketing grow in prominence, I think we will see a diminished focus on marketing to Gen Z or future generations. Gen Z promises to be even more diverse and difficult to define in any singular manner than the Gen Y (or millennial) generation already is, and many brands are finding more success in identifying cross-generational similarities than they are in identifying their differences.

This means that millennials may be the last "targeted" generation, and Gen Z would have a very different relationship with marketers. We will have to stay tuned to determine the impacts.

What will future generations' relationship with brands be?

We've already seen a seismic shift in the way that Millennials relate to brands, and the demands that they've placed on them. Any successful brand in the future must respond to these demands and continue to adapt for future generations:

- **Remember the 8-second rule:**
  A demand that brands make it quick and easy to understand their value and relationship to the consumer.

- **Remember the importance of values:**
  A demand that brands state their values and always strive to live up to them.

- **Remember the importance of authenticity:**
  A demand to use "real" people as opposed to actors, make claims that can be truly backed up, and share advertisements that focus on the pragmatic benefits versus the impractical.

- **Remember the importance of giving consumers a voice:**
  A demand that brands engage actively and openly with consumers, and provide mechanisms for feedback and conversation.

The connected generation – Generation C

Generation X is a thing. So is Generation Z. So, what is Generation C, you ask? Well, it's not so much an age range as a group of people who share common behaviors and mindsets. As early as a *Trendwatching.com* article in 2004[65], researchers identified a group of people who are heavy adopters of digital technologies, as well as creators of digital content.

Rather than being comprised of those born between an arbitrary date range, Generation C is defined as people who interact with brands in a device- and channel-agnostic manner, and who truly benefit from the "brand as relationship" dynamic where content is created and shared.

According to the 2004 Trendwatching.com article, there were two main drivers of this (at the time) new consumer behavior:

(1) The creative urges each consumer undeniably possesses. We're all artists, but until now we neither had the guts nor the means to go all out.

(2) The manufacturers of content-creating tools, who relentlessly push us to unleash that creativity, using -- of course -- their ever cheaper, ever more powerful gadgets and gizmos. Instead of asking consumers to watch, to listen, to play, to passively consume, the race is on to get them to create, to produce, and to participate.

It's interesting to see how, even more than a decade ago, the seeds of the always-connected consumer were being planted. You can also see that this type of consumer is not just someone who *consumes*. They are also *creators* of content and participate on social media channels like YouTube, Instagram and other outlets that allow them to show off their creativity.

What does this mean for the future of brands and branding? Generation C wants to continue the dialogue and the symbiotic relationship that modern, agile brands allow them to have. Whether it's the ability to create more easily, share with others, or other activities, this group is looking for new opportunities from the brands they love.

Recap

Whether we look at generations based on their age range or their mindset, it's clear that brands need to understand the shifting behaviors of consumers, whatever way they choose to segment them.

Consumers want to be able to quickly and easily understand the value and *values* of a brand, and they want to hear authentic messages from brands. While not everyone is a content creator, brands that listen to their customers and form a natural dialogue are the ones who will be the most successful in an agile world.

16 | Conclusion

"To me, marketing is about values. This is a very complicated world, it's a very noisy world. And we're not going to get the chance to get people to remember much about us. No company is. So, we have to be really clear on what we want them to know about us."
—*Steve Jobs*

With all of the information, distractions, and competing imagery, messages, and everything else going on in the world, brands don't have much real estate in consumers' minds.

If we're going to stand out, however, we need to do something that doesn't just add to the noise.

We talked in Chapter 4 about the evolution of branding, through four stages:

1. Brand as object
2. Brand as idea
3. Brand as experience
4. Brand as relationship

From object to idea, from experience to relationship, the brand itself has become an increasingly complex entity. Likewise, consumers' relationships with brands has continually evolved. We've gone on quite a journey together, starting at the origins of branding, evolving over time as consumer needs and communications methods changed. Then, adding in the evolution of process to include agile methodology brought about by access to Big Data and many other advancements. So now what?

Gail Legaspi-Gaull of research and consulting firm Hat Trick 3C puts it this way:

> "As consumers continue to seek relevance and relationships with their preferred brands, brands, in turn, have to remember that relationships are multi-dimensional and evolve depending on what stage that relationship is in. It will no longer be enough to champion a cause or put forth an attitude that is not pulled through every brand interaction and throughout the life of the

relationship. Given the ubiquity of digital, this becomes a particular challenge.

Consumers can easily see what brands are doing (or not doing) and are thus aware of how their brands are behaving. Moreover, enduring relationships are a two-way street, so allowing or even encouraging consumers to help build the relationship will be a positive differentiator. Ultimately, the question that great brands need to keep in mind to win in the future is whether their brand's behavior is consistent with the relationship that the consumer wants to have."

Just as computer programming evolved to the Software Development Life Cycle (SDLC) and then to an agile approach, inevitably, brands will continue to evolve. While the current emphasis is on what I refer to as "brand as relationship," we will, at some point, evolve beyond this.

The agile brand will be successful in an age of continual disruption because it finds a way to *meaningfully* connect with people. That doesn't mean broadcasting marketing messages or offers, but instead that brands will recognize that their value is to solve problems in a world full of constant change.

How will brands and marketers achieve this success? They will stay agile as they embrace change as the constant and consumer engagement and attention as a continually moving target. Wendy Hagen, principal of hagen inc. describes it this way:

> *"To be successful today, brands need to have a heightened sense of situational awareness (SA). To an aviator, SA means staying acutely attuned to everything you need to know about what is going on when operating an aircraft.*
>
> *The same fundamental rules of aviation apply to today's agile brands. Maintaining good situational awareness requires pilots -- and marketers -- to be attentive, mindful and focused on what's ahead, even when things are going well."*

This need to keep things adaptable is challenging because there will never be a static playbook to follow. However, if you stay nimble, listen to your customers, and focus on your role as problem solver (not sales person) you will find success.

Staying nimble and listening to your customers means that you need to allow your brand to be shaped by your customers. Your customers are now part "product owners," to use the agile terminology. The customer experience, no longer a one-way street, means that your brand gives something, but also receives ideas, feedback, and criticism from consumers. And, instead of filing it away to discuss in a strategy meeting in the future, you need to incorporate this feedback now.

The agile brand exists as a dialogue that continues to evolve, just as society evolves, new generations become consumers, and technology shifts influence the way we interact.

There you have it. The agile brand is the next step in a process that will surely continue to evolve, but embracing that evolution while staying true to the values that define and differentiate why you do what you do will keep your brand strong.

About Greg Kihlström

Greg is currently SVP Digital at Yes&, a marketing agency in the Washington, DC region that works with national commercial, nonprofit and government clients. Previously, he was founder and CEO of Carousel30, a digital agency which was acquired in late 2017 by Yes&.

He is currently serving as Vice President on the American Advertising Federation District 2 (Mid-Atlantic Region) Board of Directors, Chair of the National Technology Advisory Council for the American Advertising Federation, and on the Virginia Tech Pamplin College of Business Marketing Industry Mentorship Board (MIMB).

Greg's first book, *The Agile Web*, was published in 2017, and discusses the changing landscape of digital marketing and customer experience. He is a regular contributing writer to

Forbes and Social Media Today and has written for The Washington Post, Advertising Age, and other publications.

He has participated as a keynote speaker, panelist and moderator at industry events around the world including Internet Week New York, Internet Summit, EventTech, SMX Social Media, and Social Media Week. He has also guest lectured at several schools including Georgetown University, American University, University of Maryland, Howard University and Virginia Tech.

References

1 Greenwald, Anthony G.; McGhee, Debbie E.; Schwartz, Jordan L.K. (1998), "Measuring Individual Differences in Implicit Cognition: The Implicit Association Test", Journal of Personality and Social Psychology

2 Amos, Candace. "12 consumer brand names that are mispronounced all the time." New York Daily News. June 25, 2015.

3 Schlosser, Eric. Fast Food Nation: The Dark Side of the All-American Meal. Harper Perennial. 2002.

4 Gonzalez, Jose. "The Value of a Company's Brand When Recruiting".

5 Hine, Samuel. "How Patagonia Became Fashion's Favorite Outdoor Brand." GQ Style. June 27, 2017.

6 Morris, Ian. "Apple Has Sold 1.2 Billion iPhones Worth $738 Billion In 10 Years." June 29, 2017.

7 McClintock, Pamela. "Box Office Milestone: 'The Lego Movie' First 2014 Film to Hit $400 Million Globally." Hollywood Reporter. March 30, 2014.

8 Redding, Dan. "The History Of Logos And Logo Design." Smashing Magazine. July 6, 2010.

9 Epsilon. The impact of personalization on marketing performance. January 4, 2018.

10 eMArketer. "US Ad Spending: The eMarketer Forecast for 2017" March 15, 2017.

11 Hiebert, Paul. "Consumer Reports in the Age of the Amazon Review." April 13, 2016.

12 Blatnik, John A. "Making Cigarette Ads Tell the Truth." Harpers Magazine. August 1958.

13 Apple. "Nike and Apple Team Up to Launch Nike+ iPod". https://www.apple.com/newsroom/2006/05/23Nike-and-Apple-Team-Up-to-Launch-Nike-iPod/ May 23, 2006.

14 "Nike Redefines 'Just Do It' with New Campaign." Press Release. Nike, Inc. August 21, 2013. Retrieved November 26, 2017.

15 Polsson, Ken. "Chronology of the Walt Disney Company." Kpolsson.com April 21, 2017.

16 Merriam-Webster Dictionary: Agile, Information last updated September 4, 2017

17 Martin, James (1991). Rapid Application Development. Macmillan. ISBN 0-02-376775-8.

18 Kent Beck, James Grenning, Robert C. Martin, Mike Beedle, Jim Highsmith, Steve Mellor, Arie van Bennekum, Andrew Hunt, Ken Schwaber, Alistair Cockburn, Ron Jeffries, Jeff Sutherland, Ward Cunningham, Jon Kern, Dave Thomas, Martin Fowler, Brian Marick (2001). "Manifesto for Agile Software Development". Agile Alliance. Retrieved 14 June 2010.

19 Rooney, Jennifer. "Applying Agile Methodology To Marketing Can Pay Dividends: Survey." Forbes. April 15, 2014.

20 Mulpuru, Sucharita. "The Arc of Technology Markets: How to Buy Technology in Pivoting, Chaotic, And Stable Market Phases." Forrester Research. November 14, 2014.

21 Palm, Patrick. "Agencies Gone Agile: Why an Agile Approach Makes Sense for Ad Agencies" Huffington Post. June 17, 2017.

22 Ahmorr, Masred. "Social Media Customer Service Statistics and Trends." Social Media Today. April 13, 2017.

23 Zac Estrada. "Buick Doesn't Need to Go Down The 'Not Your Father's Oldsmobile' Road." April 3, 2014. Jalopnick.

24 IDC. "Double-Digit Growth Forecast for the Worldwide Big Data and Business Analytics Market Through 2020 Led by Banking and Manufacturing Investments, According to IDC." October 3, 2016.

25 LPK. "In an Era of Accelerated Rebrand Backlash, Starbucks and Target Stand Their Ground." February 7, 2011.

26 Mills, Russell. "Services schedule for Tulsa's 'Mr. Oktoberfest,' Josef Hardt". KJRH-TV. Archived from the original on April 10, 2010.

27 Conley, Paul. "As Lowe's Foods employees do the chicken dance, sales rise" Food Dive. July 16, 2014.

28 Milsovevic, Marija. "Rebranded Lowes Foods Offers an In-Store Adventure." BrandingMag. November 24, 2014.

29 Matthews, Daniell. "10 Keys to Developing an Agile Branding Strategy." Business 2 Community. April 28, 2016.

30 Zuckerberg, Mark. "Building Global Community." February 16, 2017. Retreived from https://www.facebook.com/notes/mark-zuckerberg/building-global-community/10103508221158471/

31 Wagner, Daniel. "Why Corporate Values Matter, even if Not All Consumers Care." Huffington Post. February 2, 2017.

32 Ames, Eden. "Millennial Demand for Corporate Social Responsibility Drives Change in Brand Strategies." American Marketing Association.

33 Bill Vlasic (April 20, 2003). "Toyota turns edgy to grab Gen Y buyers". Detroit News.

34 George, Patrick. "Why The Olds Bought The Second-Gen Scion xB Instead Of The Youths." Jalopnik. April 14, 2014.

35 Ewing, Stephen. "Scion iA and iM rolled into Yaris and Corolla lineups for 2017." AutoBlog. May 17, 2016.

36 Frey, William H. "Diversity Defines the Millennial Generation." Brookings Institute. June 28, 2016.

37 Think with Google. "Micro Moments". https://www.thinkwithgoogle.com/marketing-resources/micro-moments/ Google. Retrieved November 28, 2017.

38 Joseph, Seb. "Coca Cola centralizes social media marketing." The Drum. October 18, 2016.

39 Keating, Gina (2012). Netflixed: The Epic Battle for America's Eyeballs. Portfolio/ Penguin.

40 Lesly, Elizabeth. "Viacom's Headache: It's A Blockbuster," Bloomberg BusinessWeek. May 5, 1997.

41 Redbox surpasses Blockbuster in number of U.S. locations". Kioskmarketplace.com, November 26, 2007.

42 De la Merced, MICHAEL J. "Blockbuster, Hoping to Reinvent Itself, Files for Bankruptcy." The New York Times. September 2, 2010.

43 Patel, Nilay. "Netflix renames DVD-by-mail service 'Qwikster,' will add video games." The Verge. September 19, 2011.

44 Bialer, Jake. "Netflix Users' Qwikster Response: Here's How People Really Feel About the Change." The Huffington Post. September 21, 2011.

45 Stelter, Brian, Nick Wingfield. "How Netflix Lost 800,000 Members, and Good Will." The New York Times. October 24, 2011.

46 Woo, Stu, "Under Fire, Netflix Rewinds DVD Plan." The Wall Street Journal. October 11, 2011.

47 Spangler, Todd. "Netflix Has 30 Original Series Today, Will Double That in 2017, Content Chief Ted Sarandos Says." Variety. December 5, 2016.

48 Goldberg, Leslie. "Ted Sarandos on Netflix Programming Budget: "It'll Go Up" From $6 Billion." The Hollywood Reporter. July 27, 2016.

49 Pendergrast, Mark (2004). For God, Country and Coca-Cola: The Definitive History of the Great American Soft Drink and the Company that Makes It (2. ed., rev. and expanded, [Nachdr.] ed.). New York: Basic Books.

50 Cohn & Wolfe. "Authentic Brand 2014: Key Findings." Cohnwolfe.com

51 Byron, Jill. "Brand Authenticity: Is It for Real?" Advertising Age. March 23, 2016.

52 Montagnini, Francesca and Roberta Sebastiani. "Co-creating value in retailing: the Eataly case". http://www.naplesforumonservice.it/uploads/files/ MONTAGNINI_CO-CREATING%20VALUE%20IN%20RETAILING_THE%20EATALY%20CASE.pdf

53 Keys, Tracey, Thomas W. Malnight, and Kees van der Graaf. Making the Most of Corporate Social Responsibility. McKinsey. December 2009.

54 Nielsen. "The Sustainability Initiative." October 12, 2015.

55 Molloy, Margaret. "7 For 2017: Predictions About the Future of Branding." January 11, 2017. CMO.com.

56 O'Brien, Sarah Ashley. "Uber fires 20 employees over sexual harassment probe." June 6, 2017. CNN Tech.

57 Isaac, Mike and Susan Chira. "David Bonderman Resigns from Uber Board After Sexist Remark." June 13, 2017. New York Times.

58 Kollewe, Julie and Gwynn Topham. "Uber apologises after London ban and admits 'we got things wrong.'" September 25, 2017. The Guardian.

59 Europish. "The Top 10 Largest European Cities." August 11, 2017. http://www.europeish.com/largest-european-cities/

60 Eleventy Group. "14 Fascinating Findings for Nonprofits on Millennial Giving and Volunteering." July 7, 2014.

61 Buck, Sebastian. "As Millennials Demand More Meaning, Older Brands Are Not Aging Well." Fast Company. October 17, 2017.

62 Enso. "World Value Index" Data gathered December 26, 2017. http://enso.co/worldvalue/

63 Horovitz, Bruce (4 May 2012). "After Gen X, Millennials, what should next generation be?". USA Today. Retrieved 24 November 2012.

64 Finch, Jeremy. "What Is Generation Z, And What Does It Want?" Fast Company. May 4, 2015.

65 Trend Watching. "Gen C" http://trendwatching.com/trends/GENERATION_C.htm February 2004.